Superstition and Religion
in early
Derbyshire History

Superstition and Religion in early Derbyshire History

Gladwyn Turbutt

MERTON

First published 2006

Published by
Merton Priory Press Ltd
5 Oliver House, Wain Avenue
Chesterfield S41 0FE

ISBN 1 898937 67 2

Printed by
Dinefwr Press Ltd
Rawlings Road, Llandybie
Carmarthenshire SA18 3YDS

The ancient stones rest heavy in the heather,
And churchyard crosses point questing to the sky;
Who made these weathered artefacts and why —
Symbolic meeting of eternity and time?

Contents

List of Illustrations

The illustration on the front cover is of the Crypt at St Wystan, Repton *(English Heritage: NMR)*.

Acknowledgements

I am grateful to the following institutions and individuals for permission to reproduce illustrations both of their property and also from their published works:

© The British Museum: Plates 13, 14.
Crown Copyright: reproduced by permission of RCHME: Plates 4, 19.
Derby Museums & Art Gallery: Plates 6, 18.
Derbyshire Archaeological Society: Plates 16, 17.
Derbyshire County Council: Buxton Museum and Art Gallery: Plates 9, 11.
English Heritage (NMR): Front cover plate.
High Peak Borough Council: Plate 9.
Sheffield Galleries & Museums Trust: Plates 2, 3, 15.
Ms Karen Frenkel: Plate 8.
Lord Edward Manners: Plate 12.

I should also like to record my gratitude to Sue Palmer (formerly of Buxton Museum & Art Gallery) who assisted me with the Buxton Museum illustrations; to Margaret Parry for her customary ability in preparing a legible copy of the text; and to Philip Riden for the final stages leading to its publication.

Gladwyn Turbutt
April 2006

Abbreviations used in the Footnotes

DAJ   *Derbyshire Archaeological Journal*

RIB   *Roman Inscriptions in Britain*

VCH   *Victoria County History*

ONE

Introduction

This study considers, in an international context, the superstitions, rituals and funeral customs of ancient Derbyshire communities and the introduction and early development of Christianity in the county up to the year AD 1000. Thereafter, the county may be regarded as having become 'Christianised', and in the Domesday Survey (1086) many of the Derbyshire manors into which the county was divided are recorded as possessing their own church and priest. This does not however mean that all pagan beliefs and practices had ceased by that date, for many lingered on amongst isolated rural communities for centuries afterwards, and a few may indeed still be recognised today in local customs (e.g. in well-dressing).

The Romans introduced to Britain the last and most civilised phase of western European pagan religion, largely adopted from the Greek pantheon, but more significantly it was under their aegis that there appeared in Britain a totally new and revolutionary religion, Christianity, which was destined gradually to supplant the spiritual beliefs and practices of the pagan world. So momentous for the subsequent evolution of European culture was this new religion that the modern era has been dated from the supposed year of birth of Jesus Christ (although the early church authorities appear to have miscalculated this important event by several years)—i.e. 'Anno Domini' (AD) whereas the time-scale for prehistoric man is measured in years 'Before Christ' (BC).

The history of the development of Christianity in Derbyshire during the first centuries of its existence is largely unrecorded, but from place-name evidence, the surviving fragments of buildings and sculpture, a few pre-Conquest charters and Anglo-Saxon chronicles it is possible to reconstruct it if only in outline. For pre-Christian pagan beliefs and practices, which governed the lives of early communities in Derbyshire for thousands of years prior to the establishment of Christianity, the problem is far greater. The prime evidence can only be archaeological, supplemented by comparisons with the archaeology of other contemporary peoples in Europe and by inferences and deductions which admittedly are hard to test. Although a picture of the developing beliefs and rituals of these early Derbyshire dwellers can only be presented as if 'through a glass darkly', we may recognise in it the gradual evolution of pagan thought and practice from the mists of remote time until

Christianity finally appears on the scene. The extent to which pagan practices and celebrations may still be recognised today is a continuing problem for those who study folklore, but the supposedly pagan origins of many colourful traditional entertainments such as morris-dancing, mumming and 'guisering' have recently been critically examined and discounted by Ronald Hutton (see Bibliography).

TWO

Paganism and Superstition

As with all attempts to interpret the mind of prehistoric man there can be no certainty about his beliefs, not only because of the absence of written evidence but also because of the dangers of imposing contemporary value judgements on a totally dissimilar society. But clues to his thinking may be gleaned from the evidence of artefacts, rituals and visual images, aided by a comparison with recorded classical religious practices some of which must have had their origin in remote times. Undoubtedly symbolism played an important part in early man's mental processes, but relatively few of his symbolic images have survived, and the interpretation of those that have presents an inviting field for bizarre and speculative theories.

We should bear in mind at the outset that the use of the term 'superstition' in the following pages implies 'credulity regarding the supernatural and the irrational fear of the unknown'. From the earliest times the actions of primitive man may be assumed to have been guided principally by instinct, emotion and observation. His overriding instinct was that of self-preservation manifested in a multitude of fears of real and imagined threats to his safety from nature and from natural forces whose motivations he was unable to comprehend. Apart from the fear of animal predators he would have feared natural phenomena such as storms, floods, thunder and lightning. His powers of observation would have taught him about the rhythmic cycle of nature: the death of vegetation in winter and its regeneration in the spring, the warmth of the sun and moisture of the rain which were necessary for the vegetation to grow. On this (he would have realised) depended the lives of animals and plants and thus indirectly his own life and those of his offspring, and he would have feared lest this all-important annual cycle might cease. Most of all—since it was the antithesis of his most powerful instinct—he would have feared death. The time had not yet arrived when the concept of an after-life along the lines of an heroic Valhalla—first recognisable in western Europe amongst Celtic tribal beliefs—was to mitigate the fear of death.

The constant uncertainties and dangers of life, and the mysterious and awe-inspiring facts of birth and death, could hardly have failed to produce a deep psychological effect on his simple and untutored mind. From whence did life come, and where did the human life-force or spirit go when he died? The effect of this mystery was probably to evoke in his imagination a primitive animism in which he attributed spirits or souls not only to all living beings but also to trees, rivers, and other features of the landscape. As a corollary of this he would have believed in a spirit world outside his own existence whose agents were responsible for controlling the processes of nature. The psychological response to such pressures was for primitive man to seek to sublimate the emotional traumas to which he was subjected by devising 'magic' rituals that gave the semblance of his 'controlling' the processes of nature so as to ensure fertility amongst living beings and vegetation, and of facilitating the transition of the spirits of the dead to the spirit world lest they should trouble him further in this life. These rituals formed a corpus of superstitious practices, and sufficed to afford collective reassurance and a degree of hope to those who participated in them.

From such beginnings we may plausibly explain the genesis of a class of priests, witch-doctors or magicians amongst primitive peoples whose business it was to carry out regular rituals which would ensure that the beneficent properties and events of nature—the fertility of the soil, the rain and the warmth of the sun required for vegetation to grow and for animals to thrive—continued from year to year, and in such manner they would seek to guarantee the well-being of their peoples. Since primitive man believed implicitly in the efficacy of magic, it was magic—and particularly what Frazer termed 'homoeopathic' or 'imitative' magic—which was called into play by witch-doctors and similar practitioners to achieve this end. On the simple principle that effects resemble their causes a ritual imitation of the desired results would—according to the principles of imitative magic—be sufficient to cause it. Applied for the purposes of healing, destroying one's enemies, growing crops or producing rain,[1] successful magicians often became men of great influence and rose to the position of chiefs and kings responsible for ensuring the prosperity of their own particular tribes. If their powers were seen to fail, they might well be deposed or killed. And since early man, like animals, had little regard for the lives of his fellows, the practice of human sacrifice to ensure the conditions required for tribal survival was commonplace.

Animistic beliefs persisted for thousands of years, and tree and river worship was common in ancient Greece and Italy. Thus Alexander the Great always made a point of offering sacrifice to the local god of any river who had 'allowed' his army passage. The Celtic Druids of Iron-Age Britain worshipped the oak tree and the mistletoe, and the old rural May Day and maypole customs originated from the practice of cutting down a tree and bringing it back to the village, thus supposedly bringing home to each house the blessing of the spirit of the felled tree. The corresponding midwinter festivity centred

---

[1] Numerous examples of applications of the principle of homoeopathic magic by primitive peoples are given by J.G. Frazer, *The Goldon Bough* (Abridged edn, 1949), 11–37.

round the Yule Log, which was also believed to have equally beneficent properties, and whose ashes were scattered over the fields to ensure fertility, a piece of it being retained to light the next year's log on Christmas Eve. Celtic peoples also worshipped local deities which they believed to be associated with springs and rivers, and the Roman name for Buxton—*Aquae Arnemetiae*—is an example of a spring dedicated to a local Celtic goddess named *Arnemetia*.

Of all the emotional experiences to which primitive man was subjected the prospect of death was the most traumatic and gave rise to a deep-rooted psychological reaction. He had observed the regular decay and regeneration of nature, and by analogy he believed that man also was destined to follow the same pattern of birth, death and re-birth, and so to secure for himself the promise of immortality. As a response to the fact of death early man developed a funerary ritual which, according to his beliefs, facilitated the re-birth of the deceased and their initiation into new life in the spirit world, while at the same time appeasing the spirits and discouraging them from returning to harm the living. In this way a cult of the dead emerged in various forms amongst all primitive societies, and these cults have constituted an important field of archaeological study in different areas of the world.

Cults of the dead reveal themselves through the evidence of ceremonial burial customs. From Palaeolithic (that is, prior to *c.*8500 BC) and Mesolithic (*c.*8500–*c.*3750 BC) times burials have been found accompanied by flint implements, shells (especially cowrie shells—thought to be symbolic of fertility—placed in different positions on the body), bone and ivory ornaments, and the skeletons are often covered with red ochre (symbolic of blood and therefore of life). The finding in different parts of the world of many headless bodies and separate skulls suggests that a cult of skulls was practised widely at this early period.[1] The use of skulls as drinking cups has been observed in Upper Palaeolithic deposits, and may be compared with head-hunting activities of primitive tribesmen in modern times. Ritual trepanning (observed from the Neolithic period in Europe) must also have had cult associations.[2] Bear skulls have also been found widely in Europe, symbolic perhaps of a desire to absorb the bear's great strength, and it may be noted that such a skull was found in the Fox Hole Cave, High Wheeldon, where Bramwell reported that 'the skull lay inverted on rocks and was covered by a flat slab, recalling the purposeful burials in stone cists, from several Continental sites, of cave bear skulls.'[3] Its position suggested a Mesolithic or Upper Palaeolithic date. Other than this single example there is no evidence in Derbyshire of

---

[1] A. Ross, *Pagan Celtic Britain* (1968), 62.

[2] See S. Piggott, 'A Trepanned Skull of the Beaker Period from Dorset and the Practice of Trepanning in Prehistoric Europe', *Proceedings of the Prehistoric Society*, vi (1940), 112–32.

[3] D. Bramwell, 'Excavations at Fox Hole Cave, High Wheeldon, 1961–70', *DAJ*, xci (1971), 1–19.

burial customs dating from as early as the Palaeolithic or Mesolithic periods.

There is increasing archaeological evidence for the careful setting aside of human skulls and long bones for religious rituals from Neolithic (*c*.3750–*c*.1750 BC) times onwards. Bone 'stacks' have been found associated with both chambered tombs and round barrows, and it seems that ancestral bones of members of important tribal groups were carefully kept in these 'bone houses' and taken out for use on ceremonial occasions. Such evidence as there may have been in Derbyshire for the segregation of different types of bone in Neolithic chambered tombs (as at Five Wells: see Plate 1) has unfortunately been destroyed by the early barrow diggers. But it is interesting to note that in a Late Neolithic or Early Bronze Age context several skulls appear to have been separately buried in the Roystone Grange barrow.[1] Bateman recorded a skull burial at Hay Top, Little Longstone, while headless burials were also recorded during the nineteenth century at four other barrows.[2] The introduction of 'bone stacks' into Bronze Age (*c*.1750–*c*.400 BC) barrows has been noted by Marsden on at least four sites.[3]

In very much later times the warlike Celtic peoples of central and western Europe practised a cult of the severed human head,[4] which features in their iconography and the classical literature relating to the period. It was perhaps an outmoded survival from Palaeolithic and later cults and had a similar rationale. Thus it was believed that the soul resided in the head of an individual and that the head could therefore exist in its own right. Hence possession of a skull was believed to give control over the deceased person's spirit, and this could be used to protect the local community. For this reason the Celts carefully preserved the skulls of their enemies either in their temples or as family heirlooms. The triumphal return of the Celtic warrior with the heads of his enemies is a familiar theme in Irish and Welsh literature. This concept is vividly illustrated in the tale of 'Branwen the daughter of Llyn' in the Welsh saga *The Mabinogion*, where we find Bendigerd Vran commanding his men to cut off his head and carry it to the White Mount in London. 'And they buried the head in the White Mount, and when it was buried … no invasion from across the sea came to this island …'.[5] The human head was therefore an object of great veneration for the Celts. In the south of France skulls have been found set into niches in stone pillars, and this macabre practice later gave rise to sculptural representations of severed heads which

---

[1] B.M. Marsden, 'The excavation of the Roystone Grange round cairn (Ballidon 12), Ballidon, Derbyshire', *DAJ*, cii (1982), 23–32; R. Hodges, J. Thomas and M. Wildgoose, 'The barrow cemetery at Roystone Grange', *DAJ*, cix (1989), 7–16.

[2] Marsden, 'Roystone Grange round cairn', 31.

[3] Ibid., passim.

[4] Ross, *Pagan Celtic Britain*, 61–126.

[5] L. Norris (ed.), *The Mabinogion* (Folio Soc. edn, 1980), 45–7.

1 Five Wells Neolithic chambered barrow.

carried over into Christian times as carved heads in the form of gargoyles or as decorative motifs over church portals (e.g. as in the pediment over the door at the Romanesque church of Clonfert, Ireland).[1]

[1] B. Cunliffe, *The Celtic World* (1979), 85.

THREE

From Superstition to Religion

Funeral rituals

With the Neolithic period, and the development of society into more precisely defined family, tribal and social groups, a new element appeared in burial rituals. This was in large measure due to the evolution of man's spiritual horizon from a purely animistic level to the concept of a polytheistic hierarchy modelled on human society controlling events and processes on earth. Thus while in earlier periods magic had been practised in the belief that the processes of nature might be controlled by man provided the correct rituals were faithfully observed, the germ of religious belief—the recognition of a superhuman controlling power to which human beings have an obligation to obey and worship—may first be recognised when man began to realise that the natural cycles of summer and winter were not in fact the result of his own magical rites 'but that some deeper cause, some mightier power, was at work behind the shifting scenes of nature'.[1] He then started to lay greater emphasis on his prayers and sacrifices to the gods and spirits, and to rely less on the efficacy of his magical rituals. From an early period there appears to have been amongst mankind what the late Professor James described as 'the conception of a transcendental order external to man and society associated with abnormal, unpredictable, inexplicable and mysterious occurrences, objects and processes in the universe and in human experience.'[2] Yet for centuries priests performed magical and religious rites simultaneously, and this confusion of thought may be seen in many of the practices of ancient Egypt and India. Gradually however the propitiation and conciliation of superhuman beings, as the essential elements of early religion, came to be widely accepted as the level of civilisation advanced, and in the course of time the concept of submission to a divine will paved the way for the establishment of the major religions in the modern world.

In Egypt, pre-dynastic simple pit graves surmounted by a heap of sand

---

[1] J.G. Frazer, *The Golden Bough* (Abridged edn, 1949), 324.

[2] E.O. James, *Prehistoric Religion* (1957), 231.

with a surrounding circle of stones, essentially similar in concept to Neolithic round barrows in Britain, rapidly developed into the great megalithic architecture of pyramids and temples with their elaborate funeral cult expressing in painting, sculpture and script the vivid belief of their people in a future life and their dependence on the will of the gods. In Mesopotamia a similar, but less elaborate cult prevailed. In each case individuals of high rank were buried with their personal and domestic possessions, and there is abundant evidence of widespread sacrificial burials of wives and servants so that they might accompany their masters to the next life. Remains of funeral feasts and other ceremonials are frequent. In the eastern Mediterranean (Cyprus, Crete and the Aegean) multiple burial in rock-cut tombs and cave fissures was common, along with domestic utensils, weapons and personal ornaments. So it was too in the western Mediterranean (Malta, the Balearic Islands and Iberia) where megalithic tombs of wide variety were used for collective family interments over a long period. In Brittany and in Britain similar megalithic tombs were constructed during the Early Neolithic period, and in Derbyshire we find the appearance in the third millennium BC of the simple and unadorned chamber tomb for selected (probably aristocratic) burials. The appearance of fire in some Neolithic contexts suggests its use in mortuary ritual—perhaps for desiccation of the body prior to tomb burial, but it was not until the succeeding Bronze Age that cremation in Britain became widespread. From this period cremation and urn burial may be observed as the standard practice right across Europe from Hungary to Britain.[1]

In common therefore with other European peoples burial ritual already played an important part in later prehistoric Derbyshire society, and we find practices which have parallels elsewhere (e.g. in Scandinavia, where many of the old customs have been recorded in the Laxdale and other Norse sagas). Rituals associated with Derbyshire burial sites concern the particular mode of burial (whether this be inhumation or cremation), the grave goods buried with the dead, and the ceremonies that took place at the site. Thus we find the Neolithic chambered tombs with multiple interments (Plate 1); the later Beaker individual interments within rock-cut graves accompanied by beakers, finely made flint weapons and implements (Plate 2); the Bronze Age inhumations with bronze grave goods, personal ornaments and food vessels (Plate 3)—later giving way to universal cremation burial in cinerary urns accompanied by a few poor artefacts of flint, pebbles, and lumps of bronze.

The Early Neolithic practice of multiple interment appears to have been preceded by the excarnation or desiccation of the bodies at special sites (as at Wigber Low), after which the bones would be collected together and buried in communal tombs. Special attention seems to have been paid to skulls and

---

[1] Ibid., 101.

2 Neolithic Beaker grave goods from Green Low, *c.*2000 BC *(Sheffield Galleries & Museums Trust).*

long bones, and these were used for subsequent ritual purposes. It is possible that those interred in such tombs were members of the local tribal aristocracies. There is evidence from some of these sites of animal sacrifices, feasting and symbolic flint and pottery offerings as part of the burial rituals. The tradition of preserving human bones survived in Greece until Homeric times.

For single inhumations in rock-cut graves or cists the practice of trussing the dead in a crouched or contracted position, with the knees drawn up to the chin, wrapping it in a skin or shroud, and then placing it in the grave

3 Bronze Age grave goods, *c.*1600 BC *(Sheffield Galleries & Museums Trust).*

(sometimes in a sitting position),[1] appears to have been common in Late Neolithic and Early Bronze Age times in Derbyshire. The binding cords have obviously not survived the passage of time, but bone shroud pins have often been found in such graves.[2] We can only guess that the arrangement of the body, as if in the uterine posture of an unborn child, was regarded as

---

[1] As with the primary interment at Parsley Hay: B.M. Marsden, *The Burial Mounds of Derbyshire* (Author, 1977), 44 (Hartington Middle Quarter, no. 9).

[2] The tradition of binding limbs after death, whose origins may date from this early period, is vividly recalled in the verse of the Ashover poet Leonard Wheatcroft who put these words into the mouth of his dying wife in 1688 (*DAJ*, xl (1918), 34):

> Instead of virgins young
> My bride bed for to see,
> Goe cause some curious Carpenter
> To make a Chist for mee.
> My bride-laces of silke
> Bestow'd on maidens meet
> May fitley serve when I am dead
> To tye my hands and feet.

symbolic of the re-birth of the deceased person in a future existence. In some cases variations in the mode of this general type of burial are noticeable: for example, the specially prepared clay bed in some Late Neolithic graves[1] or the use of fine white sand laid on the ground before food vessel and urn cremations.[2]

In many examples of individual burials from this early period we notice, first, the burial of personal possessions with the deceased which it would be unlucky for others to inherit, or which might be required for a symbolic journey to another world (following the pattern of early Mediterranean civilisations). Of the former, necklaces and rings are obvious examples, while the deposit of a beaker or food vessel, and on some occasions of hazelnuts or of joints of meat, implies the furnishing of sustenance for such a journey. Secondly, there is the fact of deliberately broken weapons (axe-heads, flint arrowheads, knives; and in post-Roman times the breaking or bending of swords) as part of the burial ritual in order to release any spirits associated with them. At Brough-on-Humber, about the middle of the second century AD, a local Celtic priest was buried just outside the town. With him were buried an iron-bound wooden bucket and two sceptres, and, as Professor Frere relates, 'the two sceptres had been intentionally bent and broken to devitalise them for the journey to the other world.'[3] In a Lincolnshire village as recently as *c*.1890 a jug and mug were apparently broken before being placed on her husband's grave by a widow 'who explained to her vicar that she had to "dead" them to release their spirits to accompany her husband.'[4]

This custom of breaking objects was widespread amongst primitive civilisations. There seems to have been a general repugnance to the idea of re-using such objects (modern examples can often be noted today), and there was a fear of being polluted by things 'contaminated' by the dead. In Egypt from pre-dynastic times pots were apparently broken at the graveside; in fourth millennium BC burials in Cyprus ceremonially broken stone vases have been found; in Mycenaen times the cup in which a toast was drunk to the deceased was broken at the tomb; while Roman burials have been found with smashed

[1] As at Liff's Low (T. Bateman, *Vestiges of the Antiquities of Derbyshire, and the Sepulchral Usages of its Inhabitants, from the most remote ages to the Reformation* (1848), 42.

[2] For example, in barrows T2 and T3 on Stanton Moor there were thick layers of fine white sand on the original ground surface (J.P. Heathcote, 'Excavations at Barrows on Stanton Moor', *DAJ*, li (1930), 3, 30). This practice has parallels in Yorkshire barrows. White sand was found under each of the triple cairns on Beeley Moor (J. Radley, 'A triple cairn and a rectangular cairn of the Bronze Age on Beeley Moor', *DAJ*, lxxxix (1969), 12); under the Harland Edge barrow (D.N. Riley, 'An early Bronze Age cairn on Harland Edge, Beeley Moor, Derbyshire', *DAJ*, lxxxvi (1966), 31–53) and in Hob Hurst's House (T. Bateman, *Ten Years' Diggings in Celtic and Saxon Grave Hills in the Counties of Derby, Stafford and York, from 1848 to 1858; with notices of some former discoveries, hitherto unpublished, and remarks on the crania and pottery from the mounds* (1861), 87–8).

[3] S. Frere, *Britannia: a History of Roman Britain* (1978), 342.

[4] L.V. Grinsell, 'The breaking of objects as a funerary rite', *Folklore*, lxxii (1961), 489.

amphorae which have been used to pour libations.[1] It may not be too fanciful to see the ceremonial custom in England, whereby the Lord Chamberlain breaks his staff of office on the death of the sovereign, as one of the last remnants of this primitive ritual.

Thirdly, and more persistent throughout history, there is the constant association of the dead with objects of flint—knives, scrapers, flint chippings, and quartz pebbles. Flint was widely regarded as an effective means of confining the spirits of the dead to their graves,[2] and flint chippings have often been found in Derbyshire associated with inhumations and also in burial urns. All the evidence suggests that there was a ritual scattering of objects like flint, bones or pebbles on the grave or funeral pyre, some kind of funeral feast, and the covering over of the remains of the burial with a stone, earth or turf cairn. The sequence of such rituals cannot at present be determined, although the finds from some excavations—for instance the bones of domestic animals like the pig, sheep or ox close to the burial—point to a feast prior to the raising of the cairn. The frequency of infant burials with women suggests the possibility of infanticide on the death of the mother, and infant burials alongside male inhumations point to sacrifices.

We may gain a general, although no doubt romanticised, idea of primitive heroic funeral rites from the earliest written sources dating from Homer's time onwards. The customs described probably owed much to the traditions of earlier prehistoric practices in Europe. The general theme of the obsequies of an early warrior hero is that of the disposal of the body on a funeral pyre, accompanied by the various rituals (such as casting objects on to the fire); the quenching of the flames (with wine during the epic Greek period); the gathering together of the burnt bones into a vessel; and—as the final act—the covering of the vessel by a burial mound. Thus Achilles buried his friend Patroclus in the *Iliad*, while Aeneas goes through similar rituals in the *Aeneid*. Considerably later Beowulf is treated with a markedly similar ritual at his funeral. Herodotus, Caesar and Tacitus all describe the customs of tribal cremations which follow the same general pattern.[3] We also learn from Plutarch that under Solon's laws (*c.*600 BC) Athenians were forbidden to sacrifice an ox at the graveside, which clearly confirms the earlier existence of such a practice.[4]

---

[1] Ibid., 476–87.

[2] S.O. Addy, 'House-burial, with examples in Derbyshire', *DAJ*, xli (1919), 160–1.

[3] P. Ashbee, *The Bronze Age Round Barrow in Britain* (1960), 179–83.

[4] Plutarch, *The Rise and Fall of Athens* (ed. Ian Scott-Kilvert) (Folio Soc. edn, 1967), 43. The tradition of funeral wakes is of immense antiquity. We have just recorded the customs practised by the Gauls and Anglo-Saxons. Consider now a description by the distinguished broadcaster and journalist, Kate Adie, of a funeral wake following an Armenian Orthodox Christian burial in the 1990s—some 2,500 years later. She describes how, after the deceased had been interred, the family all assembled for a picnic round the grave, produced bottles of wine and brandy, a huge

The Derbyshire burial rite which persisted longest was that of throwing flint and pebbles on to the grave. Quartz pebbles, for example, seem to have been associated with both inhumations and cremations from Late Neolithic times,[1] and as late as the seventh century AD an Anglian grave revealed a skeleton holding a quartz pebble.[2] This superstition was still current in the sixteenth century, for Shakespeare wrote in *Hamlet* (describing Ophelia's burial): 'shards, flints and pebbles should be thrown on her'.[3] And even today we can still recognise traces of this pagan ritual in 'The order for the Burial of the Dead' set out in the Anglican Prayer Book, where the words of the rubric state:

> *Then, while the earth shall be cast upon the body by some standing by*, the Priest shall say ' ... we therefore commit his/her body to the ground; earth to earth; ashes to ashes; dust to dust; in sure and certain hope of the Resurrection to eternal life, through our Lord Jesus Christ ... .'

It would not be surprising if occasional Christian interments in Derbyshire were found to contain quartz pebbles, although this association has yet to be observed.

Concepts of the after-life

Prehistoric man's conception of an after-life is difficult to interpret because of its apparent inconsistency. Where there is found to be a strong tradition of preserving the body of the deceased—in a stone tomb or in mummified form, for example—there would seem to have been a general presumption that the departed spirit was believed to undergo a continuation of the present form of

---

'mourning cake' with a large chocolate cross on it, and eventually someone got up and made a speech, proposed a toast to the deceased, after which they all drank his health and threw the remains of the contents of their glasses on to the grave. 'And they packed up their baskets and very casually walked away. And they turned round and they *waved*.' (Bel Mooney, *Devout Sceptics* (2003), 17–18).

[1] A Beaker burial on Elton Moor was discovered with three quartz pebbles within the beaker (Marsden, *Burial Mounds*, 34 (Elton No. 1)). A secondary urn burial within a primary Beaker grave contained quartz pebbles also (ibid., 42 (Grindlow No. 1)).

[2] Ibid., 31 (Eaton & Alsop No. 4). Was it coincidence, one may wonder, that a sixth-century Anglian cremation found at King's Newton 'was very remarkable for having a large admixture of small, pure white quartz pebbles thickly intermixed with the paste of which it was composed' (J.J. Briggs, 'Notice of a discovery of ancient remains at King's Newton, Derbyshire', *The Reliquary*, ix (1868–9), 3)?

[3] Hamlet, Act 5, scene 1. As Grinsell impishly remarked, this 'poses the problem whether pre-Christian burial rites were the privilege of those who were denied Christian burial' (Grinsell, 'Breaking of objects', 489).

physical existence in another world, linked in some way to the present one, particularly as the bodies were accompanied by their personal possessions and were supplied with the means of sustenance (in the form of food and drink) on the journey to the next world (even to the extent of a reindeer sometimes being killed by the people of Lapland on the grave of the deceased so that he could ride it during the journey).[1] Yet in Egypt, where mummification reached its greatest perfection, the souls of the righteous were thought to join Osiris in a heavenly realm, and logically the ritual of cremation—which was not in fact practised—would have been a more appropriate vehicle for such a transition. Similarly the higher classes of the Peruvian Incas, who also practised mummification, were believed to pass at death to a spiritual home in the sun.[2]

On the other hand, where cremation was the general rule the implication is that of the survival of life in another—but essentially spiritual—form; hence giving credence to the theory of the transmigration of the spirit either to another physical entity in this world (i.e. reincarnation), or alternatively to a new spiritual world altogether—for example, to a 'land of heroes' in celestial realms. In this latter concept fire is seen as a 'spiritualising agent'—in both sacrifices and cremations—for the liberation of the human spirit. For this reason cremation later came to be regarded as a more certain method of protecting the living from molestation by the dead, and this belief persisted in Derbyshire until as late as the twelfth century, as is illustrated by the legend of the 'Devil of Drakelow'—in which exhumation and burning apparently ended repeated ghostly hauntings.[3] There may also have been an element of class distinction in the type of burial. Inhumation—whether collection of the bones (after excarnation) in communal burial chambers or individual burial within stone cists—may have been the rite accorded to important members of society because it preserved their identity (and in the case of collected bones these could be used for tribal rituals by future generations), whereas cremation was symbolic of the destruction of physical

---

[1] Grinsell, 'Breaking of objects', passim.

[2] James, *Prehistoric Relgion*, 132.

[3] C. Kerry, 'S. Modwen and "The Devill of Drakelow"', *DAJ*, xvii (1895), 57. A similar episode is recounted in the thirteenth-century *Laxdaela Saga* when during the tenth century in Iceland a certain Hrapp, for some time after his death, physically assaulted local people. 'Next morning Olaf went to the place where Hrapp had been buried, and had him dug up. Hrapp's corpse was still undecayed. After that he had a pyre built, and Hrapp was burned on it and his ashes were carried out to sea. From that time on no one ever suffered any harm from Hrapp's hauntings' (*Laxdaela Saga* (Folio Soc. edn, 1975), 93). T.C. Lethbridge (*The Painted Men* (1954), 82), on the other hand, cites a case of decapitation during the late Roman period which may have resulted from a fear that the ghost of the deceased person might haunt the living. Decapitated burials were not uncommon in Roman times, and a number have recently been found in the Romano-British cemetery outside the Roman fort at Little Chester (see H. Wheeler, 'The Racecourse Cemetery', *DAJ*, cv (1985), 222–80).

identity and hence was more likely to have been the appropriate rite for the great majority of society.

Fertility and hunting rituals

From the Palaeolithic period may be dated hunting rituals, the subject of many parietal paintings in France and Spain. Animals such as the bison and deer were the basis of man's food supply at that date, and rituals were aimed both at increasing their numbers as well as ensuring success in hunting expeditions. So far as the latter is concerned, cave paintings illustrate the homoeopathic magical purpose of the rituals with scenes of hunted animals depicted with arrows and spears in their bodies. There are also many representations of masked men (masks being believed to give their wearers supernatural powers to acquire the attributes of the beasts they imitated) taking part in ritual dances—possibly enacting a drama which they believed would thereafter happen in practice and thus ensure their success in the chase. The carving on a piece of reindeer rib of a masked figure holding a bow, and possibly performing a ceremonial dance, which was found at Pin Hole Cave at Creswell Crags in Derbyshire is an example from the Upper Palaeolithic period of this type of homoeopathic ritual, and a recently discovered (2003) series of engravings of an ibex, bison, horse and birds—dating perhaps from *c.*10,000 BC—in the Church Hole Cave at Creswell Crags suggests that further examples of cave art—possibly with homoeopathic ritualistic hunting scenes (as in southern France)—may be brought to light in due course.

After the predominantly hunting economy of the Palaeolithic period the economic basis of life gradually changed to one of food growing and stock rearing. This new agricultural economy of Neolithic society in turn demanded the formulation of magic rituals designed to promote the fertility of crops and ensure the continuing warmth of the sun and sufficient quantities of rain. Hence rituals developed which were related to the annual agricultural cycle of seed sowing, germination and harvesting. An interesting survival of one of these animistic rituals is the traditional cutting of the last sheaf of corn at the harvest by a village elder, from which (until comparatively recently) 'corn dollies' were made. These dollies (derived from the word 'idol') were supposed to preserve the spirit of the corn during the winter, and the following spring they would be broken up and mixed with the seed corn so as to transfer the spirit again into the soil and ensure a good harvest. The corn dolly developed into a regional art-form, with distinctive designs in different parts of the world (and indeed in different parts of Britain).

The rise of polytheism

With the gradual shift in emphasis away from the primitive animistic and magical rituals a polytheistic religious mythology began to evolve. This was based on the concept of a great 'Mother Goddess' embodying the reproductive capacity of all aspects of nature. She in turn was associated with a youthful vegetation god with whom she had intercourse each year in order to bring forth the fruits of the soil, and who annually died and then rose again from the dead in order to ensure the continuing propagation of nature. This accounted for the recurrent annual cycle of birth, death and resurrection, and of the common belief in a virgin mother goddess giving birth to a divine child which symbolised both the annual regeneration of all vegetation and the return of the sun from its winter decline. Representations of a goddess with a child on her knee, with figures paying homage to it, may be seen (for example) on a Babylonian cylinder-seal and on a Mycenaean signet ring (*c.*1500 BC) more than a thousand years before the birth of Jesus Christ.

The 'Mother Goddess' cult was first manifested in the civilisations of the Near East. In Egypt, the cult of Osiris (the god of vegetation) and his consort Isis, associated with the vital powers of the sun and of the river Nile, was pre-eminent. As Frazer points out: 'in art the figure of Isis suckling the infant Horus is so like that of the Madonna and child that it has sometimes received the adoration of ignorant Christians.'[1] In Mesopotamia, Ishtar (the 'Mother Goddess') and her consort Adonis were venerated. A 'Mother Goddess' was also the centre of worship in the eastern Mediterranean countries—e.g. in Cyprus, Crete and Greece. In Greece the earth-mother Demeter had as her consort the Indo-European sky-god Zeus, symbolising the union between the earth and the heavens which gave rise to the growth of all vegetation on earth.

Local mythology therefore in both the Near Eastern and Mediterranean countries focused on the death and resurrection of a youthful vegetation god (e.g. the Syrian Tammuz or Adonis, consort of Ishtar; the Phrygian Attis, consort of Cybele;[2] and the Greek Zeus, consort of Demeter) who was responsible—through intercourse with his earth-mother consort—for renewing the life of all vegetation in the annual cycle of nature, and ceremonial rituals were enacted to ensure that this cycle continued. Of such a nature was the celebrated Eleusinian 'mysteries' of the goddess Demeter, whose priests were members of a special caste of the highest social standing.

From the Neolithic period therefore we find throughout Europe figures

---

[1] Frazer, *Golden Bough*, 383.

[2] Themistocles, when an exile in Asia Minor, believed he saw 'Cybele the Great Mother' in a dream, and built a temple in Magnesia in her honour (Plutarch, *The Rise and Fall of Athens* (ed. I. Scott-Kilvert) (Folio Soc. edn, 1967) 92).

with exaggerated female sexual attributes, wall paintings and engravings on bone and horn of fertility dances, fertility amulets, cowrie shells and phallic emblems. In the Mediterranean region, introduced probably from Asia Minor to Crete in the first instance, and spreading thence to Greece, Malta, Iberia and finally to north-west Europe, traces of a cult of the 'Mother Goddess' with the role of earth-mother and goddess of vegetation may be observed. In north-west Europe this cult is recognised by its symbolism: the double-axe (such as those which are carved on some of the stones at Stonehenge, on a barrow stone in Dorset, and in a stone cist at Crinan, Argyllshire), the snake, the dove, the horned ox, and female figurines (for example, the stylised 'Mother Goddess' figures which have been found carved on the orthostats of passage graves in Ireland and Britain, and the fertility figurines which have been unearthed at a number of Neolithic sites). Possibly this cult flourished most strongly in Britain amongst the tribal communities living in the vicinity of Avebury, and Michael Dames has constructed an ingenious theory that the complex of monuments in that area was designed to be understood as a sequence of visual images of the 'Mother Goddess', in much the same way as a medieval passion play.[1] The cult of the 'Mother Goddess' and her consort was widely observed throughout the provinces of the Roman Empire, and for a considerable period survived the official establishment of Christianity in the fourth century AD.

The 'Mother Goddess' cult in Britain may also have been supplemented by a cult of the sun, perhaps encouraged—if not actually introduced—by the Beaker people at the end of the Neolithic period. Sky-god worship was well developed in Europe at this time: the Indo-European Zeus was worshipped in Greece, and Woden (of Indo-European origin) in Scandinavia. In Britain sun amulets of gold and amber from the Bronze Age have been found in Wessex graves, which are suggestive of a cult of sun worship. Hecataeus of Thrace, writing in the fourth century BC, referred to an island west of the land of the Celts—which could well have been Britain—in which Apollo was worshipped. Here (he recorded) there was a sacred enclosure dedicated to the god, as well as a circular temple (which could have been a reference to Avebury or to Stonehenge).[2] The later Celtic god Grannus, to whom dedicatory inscriptions have been found in Scotland and elsewhere in Europe, was regarded by the Romans as identical to Apollo.[3]

Neolithic henge monuments in Derbyshire, such as Arbor Low (Plate 4) and the Bull Ring (Dove Holes), are situated close to prehistoric trackways and were essentially focal points for local communities, at the same time as serving

[1] M. Dames, *The Avebury Cycle* (1977).

[2] J.E. Wood, *Sun, Moon and Standing Stones* (1980), 4, 199.

[3] Frazer, *Golden Bough*, 611.

4 Arbor Low henge monument from the air *(Crown Copyright)*.

as centres of ritual and ceremony in connection with the dead. Circles are believed to have had a magical connotation—which could have excluded or confined ancestral spirits—and they were a symbolic configuration both for places of burial (as at the Stanton Moor necropolis) and for sites of ceremonies and superstitious rituals. They may also have been used by a priestly class for astronomical observations connected with the formulation of a calendar and hence with the seasons and cycles of husbandry.

After the Neolithic henge monuments were deserted, ritualistic activity appears to have continued at a large number of smaller stone circle sites—mostly situated on the gritstone moorlands and contemporary with Middle and Late Bronze Age cremation urn burials. The 'Nine Ladies' circle on Stanton Moor (Plate 5) is a representative example. They suggest that society in the Middle Bronze Age period was beginning to disperse into small

5 'Nine Ladies' circle on Stanton Moor.

tribal units, and that each tribe had its own circle for communal assembly and rituals. That dancing was part of these rituals is suggested by the legend attaching to the Stanton Moor circle. Here the 'King Stone' standing nearby and the circle of nine standing stones (originally probably eleven) is held to have represented a pagan priest and group of maidens taking part in some ancient rite and being turned to stone by a disapproving Christian priest!

Celtic deities, festivals and practices

Iron Age Celtic tribes arrived in Derbyshire from the Continent from *c.*600 BC onwards. They were a remarkably vigorous people, but unlike the heroic figures of Greek and Roman antiquity they had no chronicler to record their individual exploits for posterity. All we are left with are the heroic sagas written down from oral tradition, a fanciful blend of fact and myth, and of which the late Celtic Arthurian romances are the best known in Britain. Nevertheless there are frequent references to the qualities of the Celts as a race in the works of classical writers like Posidonius, Caesar and Tacitus. All agree they were fearless, impetuous and boastful. They were expert horsemen, as well as skilled breeders of horses, and used the two-wheeled chariot with great effectiveness in warfare. But like many brave warriors of independent spirit they were ill-disciplined and their tactics unco-ordinated, so that they eventually succumbed to the relentless pressure of the highly disciplined Roman army.

The Celts worshipped numerous gods. A tribal god could be represented in a number of ways, such as a hunter or as a riding warrior god, and each locality had their own versions. They believed that the number three was equated with power, and their gods were often therefore depicted in triple form (e.g. the 'Three Mothers' shown as seated deities accompanied by emblems of fertility). When fighting, their unit was the *Trimarcisia* composed of a nobleman with his two supporters. Celtic goddesses are recognisable as a reflection of an earth mother-goddess, while the male gods are of the nature of a tribal god. The great male god was the *Dagdá*—supremely competent in every aspect of tribal life. His female counterpart was the *Mòrrigan* ('the great goddess')—a mother-goddess and goddess of fertility. At the Celtic festival of Samhain (1 November) the tribal god and earth-mother came together and their intercourse ensured the renewal of the fertility of the land.

One of the best attested Celtic cults was that of a horned god, and in Gaul there is considerable evidence for the cult of the stag-god *Cernunnos*, who is depicted wearing a torc and is associated with a ram-horned serpent. Regarded as god of the underworld, his horned appearance gave rise to the medieval representation of the devil. The torc was supposed to provide magical protection, as well as being a symbol of aristocracy. A number of representations of a *Cernunnos*-type god date from the Romano-British period. The Brigantes (whose territory embraced the northern parts of Derbyshire) worshipped a horned god who is depicted either as an armed warrior or alternatively as Mercury (regarded as protector of herds and flocks, and an example of which may be seen in the sculptured stone from Little Chester: see Plate 6).

The Romans looked for the same attributes in the Celtic deities as they accorded to their own gods and then equated the two. It is clear that, after the Roman occupation, a number of Celtic warrior gods—such as *Cocidius* or *Belatucadros*—became equated with Mars, the Roman god of war. Thus the local deity *Braciaca*, worshipped in Derbyshire, was transformed into *Mars Braciaca* where he features in a Romano-British dedicatory inscription found at Haddon (see below). Birds were of special significance to the Celts as symbols of divinity—for example the swan, raven (often depicted as a bird of ill-omen), crow, goose, owl and eagle, and they frequently feature in Celtic folk tales. It is interesting to note how Celtic ornithological superstition—such as the behaviour of birds indicating the outcome of events, their powers of prophecy, and their use as divine messengers, were taken over and adapted by the early Christian Church (which had a remarkable astuteness for transmuting pagan festivals and practices into those of its own). The use of the

6 Bas-relief of (?)Mercury from Little Chester *(Derby Museums & Art Gallery).*

dove and eagle, for example, may be followed in Christian iconography from the earliest years. Animals, too, were also of significance to the Celts, and folk tales often recount the ability of gods to turn themselves at will into animals. We find bulls, sacred cows, cats, boars (the Celtic cult animals *par excellence*, and often featured on Celtic helmets—a practice continued by succeeding Anglo-Saxon tribes), horses (a common motif on coins), stags (e.g. the antlered god *Cernunnos*), dogs, and indeed fish, in the iconographic record.

In the first millennium BC Celtic peoples throughout Europe were widely associated with fire festivals, and Celtic priests—or 'Druids'—in Britain are believed to have practised fertility and fire rites at their major festivals. Of these the most celebrated was the great spring festival of Beltane (1 May) or 'May Day'. Beltane fires were kindled right across Europe, and there are records of rituals practised in parts of Scotland until as late as the end of the eighteenth century. The eve of May Day was known in central Europe as Walpurgis Night, when witches were supposed to travel abroad, and it was the purpose of the fires to drive away the witches and evil spirits. A number of surviving rural customs consist of the burning of effigies on the fires, and there can be little doubt that these symbolise the supposed original human sacrifices of witches and other evil doers made at such times by the Druids.

May Day celebrations in Britain are recorded from at least as early as the thirteenth century and take many forms. The essential component of 'bringing in the May' (as it was called) was for young girls to fashion garlands from local flowers which were then paraded through the villages. Maypole dancing was also widespread on that day and took place on many Derbyshire village greens until recent years. Thanks to writers such as Thomas Hobbes (1568–1679) it was surmised that the maypole was a symbol of phallic fertility, and that it was originally danced round by the villagers as part of a fertility ritual. There is however no historical evidence for this: while it may have been symbolic of bringing home to the village the blessing of the spirit of the felled tree which provided the maypole, it was more likely to have been regarded simply as a symbol of the happy return of spring and of the renewed growth of vegetation, both of which were cause for celebration. By the nineteenth century it had become customary for children to dance round the pole holding different coloured ribbons, and their individual dance movements wound the ribbons round the pole in a distinctive pattern (Plate 7).

Also associated with May Day festivities in Britain was the concept of the 'Green Man', which has a direct link with traditional European and Near Eastern fertility rites going back into remote antiquity. In many local ceremonies the 'Green Man'—a wooden frame covered with straw bedecked with branches of flowers and leaves—is paraded round the village (rather as the image of a saint is carried round a Continental town on the patronal festival), after which he is ritually 'sacrificed'. In this we can recognise a clear analogy with the mythology of the death and resurrection of Near East

7 Maypole dancing at Ogston, *c.*1900.

vegetation gods such as Adonis and Attis which were designed to perpetuate the annual cycle of nature.

In Derbyshire the Castleton Garland Day ceremony almost certainly had its origins in a 'Green Man' ritual, although ostensibly it now commemorates the Restoration of Charles II and the 'King' and 'Queen' taking part both dress in clothes of the Stuart period. In the Castleton ceremony, held on 29 May (Oak Apple Day), the 'Garland King' rides on horseback (traditionally a fine shire horse with white fetlocks) beneath a garland of flowers and leaves (constructed on a wooden frame and weighing some 56 lb.), followed by the 'Queen' on another horse and then by a band and girl dancers dressed in white (Plate 8), after which the garland is lifted from the King's shoulders and hauled to the top of the church tower where it hangs until the end of the week. The procession then moves to the village green where the girl dancers (although formerly male Morris dancers) perform the traditional Castleton dances to the music of the 'Garland Tune' (originally played by two fiddles and a flute).

The 'Garland King' ceremony is in fact an uniquely curious conflation of several historic seasonal rituals. Its wooden-framed 'garland' of flowers is a direct descendant of those garlanded frameworks which were paraded

8 Castleton Garland Day *(Karen Frenkel).*

through the streets in late medieval times as part of the annual ceremony of 'bringing in the May' (condemned by Bishop Grosseteste of Lincoln in the early years of the thirteenth century), and which in turn could well have had a pre-Christian origin. It became conflated during the late eighteenth or early nineteenth century with a local rush-bearing ritual in which the local bell-ringers formed part of the parade which contained both a rush cart and the garland, and which called in at various houses in the village for hospitality (as do their successors today). By the nineteenth century the rush cart had been dispensed with and 'the procession was led by a man in ribbons and another, representing a lady in a bonnet, and consisted principally of a morris performed by the ringers'. By the end of the century the whole procession appears to have been turned into a tourist spectacle, with the 'King' and 'Queen' (since 1955 played by a woman) being dressed up in Stuart costumes appropriate to the Restoration of 1660, with all its accompanying revelry, but the bell-ringers and morris dancing have given way to schoolgirls in white dresses decorated with flowers and sprigs of oak and carrying garland sticks who march to the strains of the 'Garland Tune' played by a silver band.[1]

[1] R. Hutton, *The Stations of the Sun* (1996), 293–4; C. Porteous, *The Ancient Customs of Derbyshire* (1962), 5–7. For an account of the most recent celebration see Bonnie Yuill, 'The Garland King', *Derbyshire Life and Countryside* (May 2003), 53–4.

Public house names such as 'The Green Man' or 'Jack-in-the-Green' are still found throughout the county, and The Green Man and Black's Head Hotel at Ashbourne is one of the best known in Derbyshire.

The second great Celtic festival was the autumn festival of Samhain (1st November) which signalled the end of summer and the beginning of winter, and heralded the start of the Celtic New Year. It was regarded as a time when the spirits of the dead were supposed to visit their former homes and the living could seek their advice and guidance on the course of events during the following year. Moreover it was the season (as with Walpurgis Night) when witches were supposed to ride the skies, and evil spirits could be abroad whose activities could be deterred by the lighting of fires. The Christian festival of All Saints intended to honour all those who had been martyred under pagan Roman emperors was celebrated on 1st November, while the feast of All Souls—to pray for the souls of the dead—followed on 2nd November. It was customary in medieval days for prayers to be offered in church on either of these days for the comfort of souls in purgatory and thereafter for the bells to be rung until midnight. The feast of All Saints—known in medieval days as All Hallows—was thus designed to coincide with, and suppress, the pagan festival of Samhain, but in practice the pagan celebration came to be held on the eve of All Hallows—which became know as 'Hallowe'en', and developed into a popular family event. As part of the Hallowe'en revelries it soon became customary for mummers or 'guisers' to dress up and take the part of malignant spirits, and to provide lanterns for themselves by hollowing out grotesquely carved turnips and pumpkins and placing a lighted candle within. The present-day popularity of Hallowe'en owes much to the Irish immigration into the USA in the nineteenth century, which resulted in its becoming a national American festivity. The former widespread practice of lighting fires at Hallowe'en and praying for the souls of the dead in purgatory appears to have been a continuation of the original pagan tradition of Samhain fires, and in the village of Findern it was formerly the custom on 'Tindles Day' (2 November or All Souls' Day) for children to light fires or 'tindles' amongst the gorse on the common (that is, until its enclosure in the nineteenth century).[1] Hallowe'en is therefore a remarkable blend of a Christian feast of the dead with pagan celebrations to mark the end of the summer and to commune with the spirits of the ancestors.

The last group of Celtic immigrants to reach Britain were the Belgae who arrived from north-east France and Belgium from the late second century onwards. They had a well-defined social hierarchy, with an aristocracy possessed of personal wealth (e.g. gold torcs—one of the marks of leadership, weapons, armour, chariot fittings) and supported by a farming peasantry, and

---

[1] Hutton, *Stations of the Sun*, 373; W. Holden, 'Tindles', *DAJ*, lxv (1944), 86–8.

with an influential priestly class known as 'Druids'.[1] Popular imagination, encouraged by the speculations of eighteenth-century antiquaries like William Stukeley, assumes that 'Druids' were accustomed to perform ceremonial rituals at the Arbor Low henge, the 'Nine Ladies Circle', and at other prehistoric Derbyshire sites. Yet the period at which archaeological evidence suggests Arbor Low was being used for ritual purposes pre-dates the Celtic Druids by more than a thousand years, and artefacts found within the burial mounds of north-west Derbyshire clearly demonstrate that the burials themselves took place centuries before the appearance of Celtic people in Britain.

The absence of surviving evidence from the Iron Age points to the desertion of the older Bronze Age ceremonial sites by the end of the second millennium BC, and so far few traces have been found of Celtic cult sites, although many native sites—such as that of the goddess *Arnemetia*—must formerly have existed throughout the Derbyshire countryside. It may not be coincidental that seven stone heads have been found over the years in the Glossop area which may have been related to some vanished cult centre.

In the years before the arrival of the Romans the Celtic Druids are likely to have practised primitive magic rituals to ensure the fertility of nature and to banish evil spirits, while at the same time there were numerous local deities to whom sacrifices and offerings would be made, and some of whom were later to be associated with the major gods of the Roman pantheon. Many local deities were associated with rivers and springs (e.g. *Arnemetia* at Buxton), and this gave rise to the practice of 'well-dressing' in Derbyshire in order to propitiate the local water deity so as to ensure that water would continue to flow from the spring even during the driest of seasons.

As part of their desire to stamp out pagan practices the early church authorities forbade the worship of 'trees, fountains or stones'. Yet the practice could not be stamped out in the countryside and the medieval church was continually exhorting its parishioners against superstition. As the late Dr Moorman recalls: 'The medieval village was full of superstition, some of which was clearly a relic of pre-Christian days. How otherwise should the Winchester Statutes consider it necessary to warn people against the dangers of worshipping stones or trees or wells?'[2] Eventually a compromise was reached whereby the springs or wells were dedicated to Christian saints and worship continued but under the patronage of the church. Thus the spring of the deity *Arnemetia* at Buxton, which gave its name to the Roman town of *Aquae Arnemetiae*, eventually became St Anne's Well and its thermal water

---

[1] Few groups of people can have attracted to themselves such a mythology as have the Druids. What is known—and imagined—about them is vividly set out by Professor Stuart Piggott in *The Druids* (1968).

[2] J.R.H. Moorman, *Church Life in England in the Thirteenth Century* (1946), 82.

became renowned for its healing properties. The Romans had constructed a bath on the site and in recent years a votive deposit to the Celtic goddess *Arnemetia*, consisting of 232 Roman coins, three bronze bracelets, and a wire clasp, dating from the first century AD through to about AD 400, has been found during building work nearby (Plate 9).[1] Another ancient spring—'B(e)a-deca's spring'—gave its name to the town of Bakewell.[2] The ecclesiastical patronage of wells may be recognised in the designation of 'Holy Wells' throughout the county (e.g. in Chesterfield (first mentioned in 1196) and King's Newton) and in specifically-named wells such as St Alkmund's Well in Derby (the saint being killed *c.*800). The adornment of springs and wells with garlands of wild flowers, which had probably persisted from Celtic times, nearly died out in Derbyshire, but appears to have been revived in the village of Tissington in the early seventeenth century during a severe drought.

From the early nineteenth century well-dressing has developed into an art-form of increasing elaboration, with framed panels of damp clay into which are pressed flowers, plants, mosses, seeds and minerals to depict the selected themes for each tableau. These were traditionally biblical texts, but in recent years they have broadened their subject matter to cover episodes such as local and national anniversaries as well as local industries and houses. It has become an attractive community craft with participants of all ages, some of whom have been involved with their village well-dressing for decades. The six wells dressed annually at Tissington have long been regarded as the showpieces of Derbyshire well-dressing (Plate 10),[3] but nowadays over 40 parishes dress their wells throughout the summer. Moreover, where wells are not available 'Taps' are now dressed.[4]

Apart from deities which presided over rivers and springs, wood spirits, elves and hobgoblins, which are commonplace in folklore, probably date from this early period, and the wood elf 'Hob Hurst' (from Old English *hyrst*, meaning a hillock or copse)[5] was notorious for his mischieviousness unless placated. A number of caves and tumuli in Derbyshire are known as 'Hob Hurst's House', and the name 'Thirst House' (from OE *thyrs*, meaning a giant or demon)[6] was also sometimes applied to caves.

Outdoor forms of ritual were common to both Celtic and Graeco-Roman

---

[1] For an account of Roman Buxton see G. Turbutt, *A History of Derbyshire* (Cardiff, 1999), i. 200–1.

[2] K. Cameron, *The Place-Names of Derbyshire* (1959), 31.

[3] For a comprehensive review of well-dressing in Derbyshire see R. Christian, *Well Dressing in Derbyshire* (Derby, 1996).

[4] See N. Wilson, *The Tap Dressers: a celebration* (2000), where the dressing of the 'Taps' in the village of Youlgreave is described. Appendix 1 summarises the method of dressing a well or tap.

[5] Cameron, *Place-Names of Derbyshire*, 687.

[6] Ibid., 697.

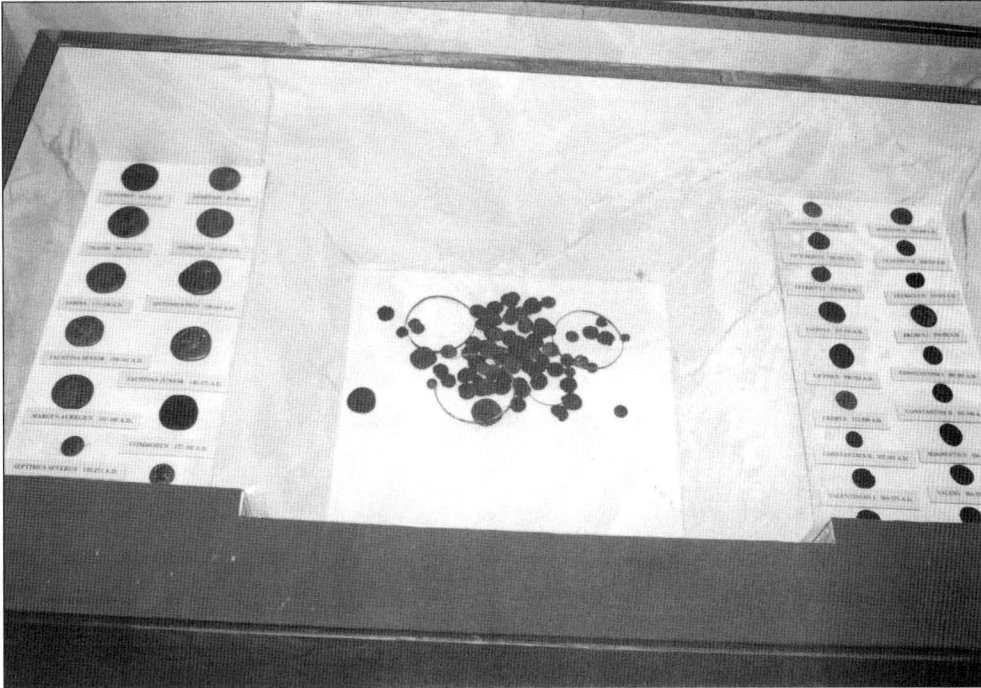

9 Votive deposit to *Arnemetia* found at Buxton *(Aquae Arnemetiae) (Derbyshire County Council: Buxton Museum and Art Gallery, and High Peak Borough Council).*

cults. Celtic religious observance usually took place in open sanctuaries or sacred woodland groves (to which the place-name element *nemeton* is often attached—e.g. *Aquae Arnemetiae*, the Roman name for Buxton, and the shrine of *Mars Rigonemetus* at Nettleham, near Lincoln), and were comparable to early Greek open-air temples. Although Celtic shrines in the form of small covered buildings are known in Britain, the practice of worshippers partaking in rituals inside sanctuaries was instituted by the early 'mystery religions' such as Mithraism and Christianity.

The Celtic belief in a material afterlife is illustrated by the type of grave goods deposited with their dead (e.g. storage vessels, cups, bowls, weapons, jewellery, and food such as joints of pork), and classical writers mention that Celts often deferred their debts to each other until they met in the next world! In the early Celtic period the poorer classes of society seem to have been cremated (a continuation of the Central European Urnfield tradition), while tribal leaders were buried within wooden chambers, complete with funeral carts and personal possessions, beneath large barrows. At a later stage inhumation for all classes, accompanied by grave goods, appears to have become commonplace. In this change one may perhaps recognise the evolution from an early Celtic aristocratic society, living an heroic existence of cattle

10 Well-dressing at Tissington.

raiding and skirmishing, while supported by a servile population of small farmers, to a less belligerent and more settled form of society. Some 200 years after the arrival of the first Celtic immigrants people of the more advanced La Tène culture from the Seine–Marne area of France began to reach Britain. Their arrival constituted a milestone in the history of Britain since before long some of their names would be the first of any British tribesmen to be found in the works of classical writers. One such tribe was the Parisi, who settled in East Yorkshire and who brought with them their traditional custom of inhumation burials within rectangular ditched enclosures (many of these have been discovered in the East Riding of Yorkshire). Rectangular ditched burials of this type have recently been found along the Trent valley (e.g. at Aston-on-Trent).[1] The Parisi also introduced to Britain Celtic La Tène art—derived from an intermixture of Greek forms and elements of the art of northern nomadic races which found in the native craft of metalworking an ideal vehicle for self-expression. This dynamic Celtic art form re-emerged when Roman influence waned in the fifth century AD and then combined with intrusive Anglo-Saxon art forms to find expression in Derbyshire in the many pre-Conquest Christian sculptured stone crosses and sarcophagi.

Greek and Roman beliefs

Within the Roman empire we can recognise two strands of superstitious and religious belief. The oldest and most personal of these, stemming directly from primitive animism, was the Roman cult of the spirits of the family and household, in particular the *lares familiares* whose worship took place in the household shrine or *lararium*, and to a lesser extent the *penates* (spirits of the larder) and Vesta (goddess of the hearth). On the same plane, and no doubt with a common origin, was the cult of the *genius loci* (or 'Spirit of the Place')—a useful substitute when the local deity's name was unknown or uncertain, and of the concept of the personal *numen* or spirit (especially that of the Emperor). Worship of the household gods was essentially a personal and family observance, binding together the spirits of the past and present members of the family. The other strand of belief was based on the earlier Greek concept of a polytheistic hierarchy of gods and goddesses dwelling on the summit of Mount Olympus under the supreme authority of Zeus, with whom the Roman god Jupiter was identified. The gods were believed to have particular human interests: for example, Mars was the Roman god of war and of all things military; Venus (the Greek Aphrodite) the goddess of love; Minerva the goddess of wisdom and the arts. They were believed to take an

[1] M. Todd, *The Coritani* (1973).

active interest in worldly affairs; could disguise themselves in human or animal form; and could have physical relationships with humans (thus Thetis, one of the Nereids, was believed to have married Peleus and to have had as their offspring the famous Achilles). The Romans took over from the Greeks the pantheon of Olympian gods and gave them Latin names (except in the case of Apollo with whom they could equate no Italian deity).

From classical times it was a recognised duty to propitiate the gods by regular sacrifices, and to consult them through the medium of soothsayers and oracles. Thus throughout the ancient world temples were built and dedicated to the various gods, and soothsayers appeared to interpret their views. The most famous was the oracle at the temple of Apollo at Delphi, in fact a group of five highly intelligent priests who purported to interpret the unintelligible babblings of an uneducated peasant woman. This oracle flourished from Mycenaean times until the fourth century AD. It was deemed essential for the support of such oracles to be obtained before embarking on any enterprise. This attitude was one which the Romans had taken over from the Greeks. 'To the Athenians, religion, both in its mythological and in its ritual aspect, was a matter of public observance, not of private belief: they used one and the same word for acceptance of the theology and observance of the rite. Both, to the traditionalist, were crucial to the survival of the state; any challenge to either was an attack on the national identity and social cohesion of the city. Hence the charge of impiety which was levelled at Anaxogoras and Socrates was not an assault on the liberty of individual conscience, but a natural, and within its own terms proper reaction to a threat to state security.'[1]

Throughout his epic campaign against the Persian empire, which took him from Macedonia to beyond the Indus during the late fourth century BC, we cannot fail to note Alexander's punctiliousness in offering sacrifices to the gods, and his frequent consultation of the omens (as interpreted by his trusted companion Aristander the seer) before undertaking any military action. So it was that when he reached the Indian Ocean Alexander 'slaughtered bulls as a sacrifice to Poseidon and flung their bodies overboard, and poured a libation from a golden cup, and flung the cup, too, and golden bowls into the water for a thank-offering, and prayed that Poseidon might grant safe conduct to the fleet … '.[2] Both Greeks and Romans also continued the pagan animistic tradition of worshipping the local river deities, as well as those of trees and other natural features. Thus after Alexander had defeated the Getae, who lived on the north bank of the Danube, he 'offered sacrifice on the banks of the

---

[1] P. George, introduction to *Plato: The Trial and Execution of Socrates* (Folio Soc. edn, 1972), 8.

[2] Arrianus, Flavius, *The Life of Alexander the Great* (trans. A. de Sélincourt) (Folio Soc. edn, 1970), 214. Alexander's custom was to sacrifice to the gods and then to hold ceremonial games for the army (see pp. 121, 194). He always took the advice of local soothsayers, and when in Babylon sacrificed to the god Bel according to the instructions of the Chaldean priests (p. 110).

Danube to Zeus the Saviour and Heracles, not omitting the River himself, for allowing the passage.'[1]

The Romans were extremely tolerant in matters of religion: the state demanded religious observance but the individual could choose (within limits) whom he worshipped. The only cults proscribed in the early period of the empire were those, like Druidism, whose practices (such as human sacrifice) were deemed contrary to civilised behaviour, or which were held to be subversive (as was Christianity in its early years).[2] The Roman attitude was

---

[1] Ibid., 27.

[2] The official Roman attitude towards Christianity is particularly well illustrated by the younger Pliny's letter to the emperor Trajan: 'I have never been present at an examination of Christians. Consequently, I do not know the nature or the extent of the punishments usually meted out to them, nor the grounds for starting an investigation and how far it should be pressed ... For the moment this is the line I have taken with all persons brought before me on the charge of being Christians. I have asked them in person if they are Christians, and if they admit it, I repeat the question a second and third time, with a warning of the punishment awaiting them. If they persist, I order them to be led away for execution; for, whatever the nature of their admission, I am convinced that their stubbornness and unshakeable obstinacy ought not to go unpunished. There have been others similarly fanatical who are Roman citizens ... Now that I have begun to deal with this problem, as so often happens, the charges are becoming more widespread and increasing in variety. An anonymous pamphlet has been circulated which contains the names of accused persons ... Amongst these I considered that I should dismiss any who denied that they were or ever had been Christians when they had repeated after me a formula of invocation to the gods and had made offerings of wine and incense to your statue (which I had ordered to be brought into court for this purpose along with the image of the gods), and furthermore had reviled the name of Christ: none of which things, I understand, any genuine Christian can be induced to do. Others ... first admitted the charge and then denied it ... This made me decide that it was all the more necessary to extract the truth by torture from two slave-women, whom they call deaconesses. I found nothing but a degenerate sort of cult carried to extravagant lengths. I have therefore postponed any further examination and hastened to consult you. The question seems to me to be worthy of your consideration, especially in view of the number of persons endangered; for a great many individuals of every age and class, both men and women, are being brought to trial, and this is likely to continue. It is not only the towns, but villages and rural districts too which are infected through contact with this wretched cult. I think though that it is still possible for it to be checked and directed to better ends, for there is no doubt that people have begun to throng the temples which had been almost deserted for a long time; the sacred rites which had been allowed to lapse are being performed again, and flesh of sacrificial victims is on sale everywhere ... It is easy to infer from this that a great many people could be reformed if they were given an opportunity to repent' (*Pliny: a self portrait in letters* (trans. and intro. by Betty Radice) (Folio Soc. edn, 1978), 241–2). Trajan replied to Pliny as follows: 'You have followed the right course of procedure, my dear Pliny, in your examination of the cases of persons charged with being Christians, for it is impossible to lay down a general rule to a fixed formula. These people must not be hunted out; if they are brought before you and the charge against them is proved, they must be punished, but in the case of anyone who denies that he is a Christian, and makes it clear that he is not by offering prayers to our gods, he is to be pardoned as a result of his repentance ... But pamphlets circulated anonymously must play no part in any accusation. They create the worst sort of precedent and are quite out of keeping with the spirit of our age' (Ibid., 242–3). The point was that all 'political societies' were at that time forbidden, and the Roman authorities believed that Christian communities were potentially seditious groups. On another occasion Pliny asked Trajan for advice on the admissibility of forming a company of firemen, limited to 150 members, in Nicomedia to deal with future outbreaks of fire in the town. But Trajan turned down the idea: ' ... we must remember that it is

essentially one of believing in a contract between the gods and the individual state: if the correct rituals were observed, the gods would offer their protection. 'The old Roman worship was businesslike and utilitarian. The gods were partners in a contract with their worshippers, and the ritual was characterised by all the hard and literal formalism of the legal system of Rome.'[1] Thus an answered prayer, where a vow had previously been made by an individual, would often be followed by the erection of an altar to the deity concerned bearing an inscription which referred to 'a vow fulfilled'. Scores of such altars are found in Britain and throughout the Roman empire, and an example which may be cited from Derbyshire is the altar dedicated to the goddess *Arnemetia* by Aelius Motio in consequence of a vow fulfilled, and found amongst the debris in the fort at Brough[2] (Plate 11).

This attitude stemmed from the belief held in the early days of the Republic that the rise of the Romans, a small Latin tribe, to the undisputed leadership of Italy and of the Mediterranean world had been predestined by the gods, and religious belief was therefore an integral part of the outlook of Roman society. As Virgil wrote:

> Tu regere imperio populos, Romane, memento
> (Hae tibi erunt artes), pacisque imponere morem,
> Parcere subiectis et debellare superbos.[3]

They were also strongly influenced by the Greek view of the public observance of religious rituals. However, by the beginning of Augustus's reign the effects of a century of civil war had produced a sharp moral and religious decline in society. Writers such as Virgil and Horace urged a return to the old virtues of public duty and religious observance which had inspired their fellow countrymen during the early years of the Republic, and Virgil's emphasis on the subordination of men's actions to the will of God was later

---

societies like these which have been responsible for the political disturbances in your province, particularly in its towns. If people assemble for a common purpose, whatsoever name we give them and for whatever reason, they soon turn into a political club … ' (Ibid., 219). From this it is clear that it was the political, rather than the religious aspects of Christianity that the Romans feared.

[1] S. Dill, *Roman Society in the Last Century of the Western Empire* (2nd edn, 1919), 75.

[2] This altar, some 20 in. high and 12 in. wide, bears an inscription in Latin which, in translation (*RIB* 281), runs:
> To the goddess Arnomecta
> Aelius Motio gladly, willingly,
> and deservedly fulfilled his vow

[3] *Aeneid*, vi. 851.

11 Altar dedicated to *Arnemetia* at Brough *(Derbyshire County Council: Buxton Museum and Art Gallery).*

seen by some as foreshadowing the coming of Christianity.[1] Augustus attempted to check the ills of contemporary society by reviving the old state religion and the virtues of family life as they had existed under the old Republic,[2] and in the early days of Roman Britain the worship of the Capitoline Triad—Jupiter Optimus Maximus, Juno and Minerva—was therefore encouraged, and temples constructed in their honour. This later gave way to the Imperial Cult, the worship of the reigning emperor in conjunction

---

[1] In *The Georgics*, for example, there is the presciently deistic passage:
  ... For God, they say,
  Pervades all things, the earth and sea and sky.
  From Him the flocks and herds, and man and beast,
  Each have the thin-spun stream of life at birth;
  To Him all things return, at last dissolved:
  There is no place for death ...
(Publius Virgilius Maro, *The Georgics* (trans. K.R. Mackenzie) (Folio Soc. edn, 1969), 76).

[2] Against considerable opposition from those long accustomed to the spirited cosmopolitan society of Rome. Indeed the poet Ovid (43 BC–18 AD), exiled for his non-conformity with the new Augustan society, wrote scathingly: 'Prisca iuvent alios: ego me nunc denique natum gratulor: haec aetas moribus apta meis' ('Let other people delight in the past: I am grateful that I was born at this time; this age suits my character').

with the goddess Roma (which is known to have been introduced to Colchester *c.*49). Thus we find records referring to the *seviri Augustales* (the group of people—usually freedmen—who conducted the ceremonies of emperor-worship in imperial towns) at York and Lincoln. In Britain the army naturally tended to favour the worship of Mars, the god of war, and there are many altars dedicated to him by imperial soldiers. But the local Celtic tribesmen had their own deities, and after the Roman occupation these often came to be identified with the more influential Roman gods. As Dill reminds us: 'The Roman soldiers were the great apostles of syncretism. Prone as they were to superstition, exposed to constant danger on the march or in distant quarters, the ingrained Roman awe of the unknown divinity made them ready to invoke the help of the guardian gods of the regions where they found themselves, and innumerable inscriptions remain to attest the liberality of their faith … '.[1] We therefore find throughout Britain a number of altars dedicated to a combined Roman–Celtic god. In Derbyshire this practice can be seen in the altar dedicated to *Mars Braciaca* which was found at Haddon. This altar (Plate 12) bore the inscription: DEO MARTI BRACIACAE Q. SITTIUS CAECILIA [NU]S PRAEF[ECTUS] COH[ORTIS] I AQUITANO[RUM] VO[TUM] S[OLVIT] ('To the god Mars Braciaca, erected by Q. Sittius Caecilianus, of the First Cohort of Aquitani, who fulfilled his vow)'.[2] Elsewhere in the province we find dedications to *Mars Rigisamus* (West Coker), *Mars Rigonemetes* (near Lincoln), *Mars Cocidius* (from the Roman Wall) and *Mars Corotiacus* (near Ipswich).

As in prehistoric days careful attention was paid by the Romans to the burial of individuals so as to ensure that the spirit of the departed was treated with due respect. Proper burial ritual was required, and commemorative rites had to be celebrated in later years. Libations poured over the grave from time to time were encouraged. 'Burial clubs' were even formed by the poorer members of society so as to guarantee the proper treatment of their members' spirits on death. There is a remarkable similarity here to the Christian practices of medieval guilds in furthering the well-being of their members' souls by the observance of proper obsequies and the subsequent offering of trentals and annuals on their behalf. The ritual practised in the case of cremation was for the body to be burnt on a pyre (sometimes with food for symbolically sustaining the deceased on his journey to the Underworld); the ashes would then be washed in wine and placed within a container (compare the ritual practised by the Greeks); and sacrifices offered to the family *lares*. Inhumations might be in a wooden, lead or stone coffin placed within a grave or more elaborate tomb. Amphorae and bowls have been found in graves, and in the case of inhumations coins are sometimes found on the bodies for the

---

[1] Dill, *Roman Society*, 95.

[2] *VCH Derbyshire*, i. 252. The First Cohort of Aquitanians was stationed at Brough and re-built the fort *c.*154 (Turbutt, *History of Derbysbire*, i. 189–90).

12 Altar dedicated to *Mars Braciaca* now at Haddon Hall (*Lord Edward Manners*).

payment to Charon for ferrying the 'shades' of the departed across the river Styx to the Underworld.[1]

It was also common for bodies to be buried in their footwear—particularly in their hobnailed boots, as if it was customary to provide such footwear for the journey to the Underworld. Examples of such burials have been found in the cemetery at Little Chester. The Romans had a strict rule that the dead could not be buried within a town, and for this reason the roads leading out of towns were often lined with cemeteries. Much importance was placed on family graves and on memorials to the dead (the likenesses of whom might be sculptured in relief on the tombs), and the five mausolea excavated at Little Chester provide examples of this practice.

---

[1] P. Salway, *Roman Britain* (1981), 704; Lethbridge, *Painted Men*, 82–3.

FOUR

Mystery Religions and Christianity

Before long new cults—particularly from the Near East—found their way to Britain. They differed from the old state religion in that they offered, not a personal contract between god and man, but a personal relationship and commitment between worshipper and his god. Amongst these new cults or 'mystery religions' were those of Isis; the 'Mother Goddess' ('*Magna Mater*') Cybele; Mithraism (akin to Iranian Zoroastrianism); and Christianity. Religious beliefs spread from the eastern Mediterranean to the West through the medium of traders, travellers and imperial soldiers. By the third century AD Mithraism (which had points of resemblance to Christianity) was popular amongst soldiers on the Roman Wall in Britain to whom its emphasis on discipline and integrity appealed. Christianity had reached Britain by the second century, where it is referred to (albeit in very general, and perhaps therefore historically unconvincing terms) by Tertullian (*c*.200 AD) and by Origen (*c*.240 AD). St Alban, a Roman citizen and reputedly the first Christian British martyr, is supposed to have died in 208/9.[1] By 312 Christian bishoprics had been established at York, London and possibly Lincoln,[2] and these sent representatives to the Council of Arles in 314.

In the early years of the Empire those holding Christian beliefs were subjected on occasions to cruel persecution, and the exemplary courage displayed by the early Christian martyrs (such as St Peter, St Paul, St Polycarp and all those who suffered during the Neronian and other persecutions) constitutes one of the most moving chapters in the history of the early church. In 313—following the defeat of his rival Maxentius—the emperor Constantine issued an edict of toleration, the now famous Edict of Milan, which forbade the persecution of all monotheistic cults within the Empire. Constantine was not however a Christian convert (only being baptised on his deathbed, when he may or may not have been aware of what was happening). The official state religion at this time was the worship of 'Sol Invictus' (the unvanquished sun) of which the emperor was the chief priest. But in Constantine's view

---

[1] Although, as explained by Professor Charles Thomas (*Christianity in Roman Britain to AD 500* (1981), 48-50), there is some considerable doubt about this.

[2] M. Todd, *The Coritani* (1973), 41–2.

religious unity, like political unity, was essential for the well-being of the state, and he was therefore prepared to tolerate any cult which appeared to harmonise with that of Sol Invictus. The popular cult of Mithraism, which also involved sun worship, taught the immortality of the soul, a future judgement, and the resurrection of the dead, was therefore regarded as complementary to the state religion. Christianity, too, another monotheistic cult which had much in common with Mithraism, was also tolerated, and Constantine was disposed to regard the deified Jesus as an earthly manifestation of Sol Invictus. His eclectic outlook thus allowed him to build a Christian church at the same time as raising statues to Sol Invictus (in his own likeness) and to Cybele the 'Mother Goddess'. The Council of Nicaea, meeting under his chairmanship in 325 to discuss Christian dogma and organisation, decided by a reassuring vote (218 in favour with two against) that Jesus was a god and not a mortal prophet (and, from the emperor's point of view, could therefore be more easily accommodated with the state religion).

Constantine's tolerant attitude ensured the establishment of Christianity in Britain, and the subsequent prohibition by Theodosius—first (in 391), of all sacrifices and the permanent closure of all pagan temples, and secondly (a year later) of the worship of household gods—further helped to increase the influence of the early Church. Constantine himself set an example by restoring destroyed churches, granting them landed endowments, and encouraging laymen to do the same. It is possible that some of the surviving wealth of pagan temples, as well as being spent by the Emperor on imperial projects and administration, was transferred to the Church at this period. Constantine also handed over the Lateran Palace to the Bishop of Rome, and this—together with the forged document known as the 'Donation of Constantine' (purporting to transfer certain of his secular powers to the Bishop of Rome)—helped to ensure the supremacy of Rome over other centres of Christian authority (e.g. Alexandria). He also (in 331) commissioned new copies of the Bible, and since most of the early Christian writings had been destroyed on the orders of Diocletian in 303 this provided a rare opportunity for the revision and re-editing of the New Testament so as to produce a new and orthodox version which could also be used to combat heresies (and which, incidentally, has remained virtually unchanged to this day).

In return for Constantine's favours the fourth-century Christian leaders were prepared to concede to the emperor the Messianic achievement which Jesus Christ had manifestly failed to deliver, and to acknowledge his priest–king status under the patronage of Sol Invictus or 'God the Father' of their faith. Indeed, Eusebius, bishop of Caesarea (c.264–340), addressing Constantine in the following terms: '... most God-fearing sovereign, to whom alone of those who have yet been here since the start of time has the Universal

All-ruling God Himself given power to purify human life',[1] comes perilously close to denying the very existence of Christ.

Religious conservatism was perhaps the most difficult obstacle for the new religion to overcome, and we have it on good authority that at the end of the fourth century the majority of the Roman Senate had shown little sympathy towards it. For them and for many of their countrymen *Roma Dea*, the idealised genius of the Latin race, was the object of their real devotion:

> Imbedded in law, language, literature, the deepest instincts of the people, her ancient worship seemed inseparable from the very identity of Rome. The true Roman, even though his religious faith might not be very deep or warm, inherited the most ancient belief of his race that the gods of a city were sharers in all its fortunes ... The complete and literal acceptance of the Christian faith seemed to mean a refusal to perform the duties of citizens or soldiers, a scornful abandonment of the old traditions of culture, even a loss of faith in the mission of Rome.[2]

This was very much the view of the emperor Julian (361–3), known as 'the Apostate', who personally renounced Christianity and while not persecuting its adherents nonetheless stripped the church of many of its privileges and openly encouraged the old state religion.

But if conservatism was a continuing problem for Christianity so too was heresy. The major early heresies—Manichaeanism and Arianism in particular—had as their common factor a belief that Jesus Christ was wholly mortal, was in no sense divine, but was an inspired teacher. They were also essentially Gnostic in outlook, believing in a mystic and experienced personal relationship with God and rejecting the need for any kind of official intercession between man and God such as an ecclesiastical hierarchy. This was a serious threat to the orthodox Roman Church, and although Arianism had been condemned by the Council of Nicaea (325) it attracted increasing support in western Europe, and elements of Arian belief were to be found as late as the thirteenth century amongst the tenets of the Cathars against whom in 1208 Pope Innocent III launched the 'Albigensian Crusade'. Other influential 'heretics' included Priscillian (*c*.340–386), bishop of Avila, who had a large following in north-west Spain and who was executed in 386 (the first person to be executed for heresy in the Church), and Nestorius (who died in 451), patriarch of Constantinople, who was excommunicated and exiled to Egypt in 435. The continuing strength and resilience of heretical opinion is illustrated by Procopius (who was born about 500) in *The Secret History* where he refers

---

[1] A. Kee, *Constantine versus Christ* (1982), 41.

[2] S. Dill, *Roman Society in the last century of the Western Empire* (2nd edn, 1919), 10.

to the many heresies then prevalent within the empire—Montanism, Sabbatarianism, Manichaeanism, for example—and goes on to state that:

> the churches of these heretics, as they are called, especially those who professed the doctrine of Arius, possessed unheard-of riches. Neither the whole Senate nor any other very large body in the Roman State could compete in wealth with these churches. They possessed treasures of gold and silver, and ornaments covered with precious stones, beyond description and beyond counting, houses and villages in great numbers, and many acres of land in all quarters of the world ... since none of the long line of emperors had ever interfered with them ....

Even allowing for Procopius's exaggeration of the wealth of these churches which the Emperor Justinian expropriated, this passage clearly indicates that the numerous 'heretical' sects had long been tolerated and some—especially the Arians—had become immensely wealthy by the mid sixth century.[1]

Christianity was subject to intense competition from other cults in its early years, and it is clear that it had to compromise and adapt in order to survive. Indeed its success against its rivals reveals an extraordinarily astute sense of what was required to appeal to contemporary popular religious imagination, and how this could be met by borrowing accepted myths and rituals from other cults. One of its rivals of long standing was the worship of Cybele, the Phrygian 'Mother of the Gods', which had been adopted by Rome in 204 BC and had achieved considerable support in parts of the Roman Empire. It can hardly be coincidental that the death and resurrection of Christ as related in the New Testament contains precisely identical symbolism to the death and resurrection at the spring equinox of the Phrygian Attis, a youthful tree-spirit or vegetation god and consort of Cybele. He, too, was said to have been born miraculously of a virgin (a not uncommon attribute of divinity in primitive societies, and often accompanied by the simultaneous rising of a star); his effigy was annually buried in a sepulchre with great mourning and lamentation; he also was held to have risen from the dead as a testimony that his disciples would triumph over the grave; and his day of resurrection—the third day—was an occasion for great celebration (the Festival of Hilaria, held on 25 March). Furthermore, the worshippers of Attis had mystical initiation ceremonies which included a sacramental meal and baptism in the blood of a bull which ensured that the novitiate 'had been born again to eternal life and had washed away his sins in the blood of the bull.'[2] According to a fourth century Christian writer, supporters of the Phrygian 'Mother Goddess'

---

[1] See Procopius, *The Secret History* (Folio Soc. edn, 1990), 53.
[2] J.G. Frazer, *The Golden Bough* (Abridged edn, 1949), 347–56.

cult bitterly attacked the Christians for having copied the death and resurrection of Attis in their new religion.[1]

The cult of the Syrian Adonis (meaning 'Lord') was in many ways similar to that of the Phrygian Attis, and the celebration of his death and resurrection was widely observed in Syria and the West about the time of the birth of Christ. As Frazer remarked:

> When we reflect how often the Church has skilfully contrived to plant the seeds of the new faith on the old stock of paganism, we may surmise that the Easter celebration of the dead and risen Christ was grafted upon a similar celebration of the dead and risen Adonis, which … was celebrated in Syria at the same season.[2]

For the new religion to be successful amongst the wide diversity of people within the Roman empire Jesus Christ had to be no less a god incarnate than his rivals such as Attis, Adonis or Osiris, all of whom were believed to have died and have been re-born in the spring, and the Christian festival of Easter (so named by Bede in the early eighth century as being derived from the pagan goddess Eostre) was deliberately made to coincide with the spring rites of these contemporary cults. Frazer interestingly speculated that the well-known representation of the sorrowful 'Mother Goddess' with her dying lover in her arms may well have been the prototype of the *Pieta* of Christian art—the Virgin with the dead body of her divine Son in her lap.

It has long been recognised that, according to the principle of homoeopathic magic, primitive man regarded the eating of the flesh and drinking of the blood of his enemies as a means of acquiring their attributes (e.g. strength, skill, or cunning). In like measure the consumption of the physical attributes of a vegetation god like Adonis or Attis—that is bread (from corn) and wine (from the grape)—would be tantamount to consuming the real body and blood of the god and thereby sharing in the god's attributes and powers. The drinking of wine at Dionysian festivals was for this reason regarded as a solemn sacrament. By the same symbolism the Christian Eucharist, in which bread and wine are consumed, would have been the most readily comprehensible sacrament to adherents of the early Christian Church. Here again, then, we have another plausible example of the pagan stock on to which a Christian ritual was grafted.

A relic of the Church's struggle with the cults of Sol Invictus and Mithraism (which had an alarming ability to absorb other cults and whose shrines are believed to have been attacked by Christians in the fourth century)

---

[1] Ibid., 361.
[2] Ibid., 345.

lies in the Christian festival of Christmas. The 25 December, being then (as reckoned by the Julian calendar) the date of the winter solstice, was celebrated by both the state cult of Sol Invictus and also by that of Mithras as the festival of Natalis Invictus (the birth of the unvanquished sun) representing the birthday of Osiris (or Aion, as he later became known). For centuries Egyptians were accustomed to watch for the appearance of the star Sirius on the horizon, for this event foretold the birth of Osiris and the rising of the waters of the river Nile. Now the Egyptian Christians were accustomed to celebrate the birth of Christ on 6 January, but according to a Syrian Christian, Scriptor Syrus, writing in the late fourth century:

> It was a custom of the pagans to celebrate on the ... twenty-fifth December the birthday of the Sun, at which they kindled lights in token of festivity. In these solemnities and revelries the Christians also took part. Accordingly when the doctors of the Church perceived that the Christians had a leaning to this festival, they took counsel and resolved that the true Nativity should be solemnised on that day and the festival of the Epiphany on 6 January.[1]

Thus Christ's nativity was made coincident with the start of the traditional festivities by which for thousands of years primitive societies had celebrated the re-birth of the sun, and whose imminent birth was signalled by the appearance of the star Sirius. He thereby assumed the place of Mithra as Sol Invictus, or, in Christian prophetic parlance, the 'Sun of righteousness', and effectively became for many the latest in a series of sun gods known by different names in many parts of the ancient world. The aureole of light which crowned the head of the sun god was soon transmuted into the Christian halo. The 'twelve days of Christmas', ending with the feast of Epiphany (6 January), coincided with the Roman festivals known as the Saturnalia (starting on 17 December) and the Kalendae (from 1 to 3 January) which were carnivals of merry-making and licence. Since holly was the emblem of the Roman Saturnalia, and ivy was associated with the Dionysiac winter solstice revelries in Greece, it is hardly surprising to find that the holly and the ivy adorned the homes of early Christians at Christmas, one of many pleasantly pagan traditions which has persisted to this day.

The New Year festivities in fact had earlier resonances, since it was long recognised that the Kalendae also represented ancient European festivals of midwinter to mark the winter solstice, whose pagan celebration was denounced by leading churchmen but which in due course came to be

---

[1] R. Hutton, *The Stations of the Sun* (1996), 1. In Anglo-Saxon times the feast of the Nativity was described simply as 'midwinter', and the term Christmas does not appear in literature until 1038 (Ibid., 6).

'Christianised' by declaring 1 January to be the feast of Christ's circumcision. The Yule Log Christmas custom (Yule being the Scandinavian word for Christmas), whereby a large log was triumphantly brought home to be lit on Christmas Eve (from a piece of the previous year's log, according to the poet Herrick) and kept burning for the 'twelve days of Christmas', its ashes being removed daily and scattered over the fields, has been regarded—perhaps somewhat dubiously—as a throw-back to the pagan midwinter fire festivals.

By a similar process of transmutation, the festival of the Assumption of the Virgin succeeded the festival of Diana; that of St John the Baptist the pagan Midsummer festival; and that of All Saints the old pagan festival known as Samhain. As Frazer concluded:

> Taken together, the coincidences of the Christian with the heathen festivals are too close and too numerous to be accidental. They mark the compromise which the Church in the hour of its triumph was compelled to make with its vanquished yet still dangerous rivals. The inflexible Protestantism of the primitive missionaries, with their fiery denunciations of heathendom, had been exchanged for the supple policy, the easy tolerance, the comprehensive charity of shrewd ecclesiastics, who clearly perceived that if Christianity was to conquer the world it could do so only by relaxing the too rigid principles of its Founder, by widening a little the narrow gate which leads to salvation.[1]

This 'easy tolerance', which enabled the fourth-century Roman to attend Mass in the morning and sacrifice to his *lares familiares* in the afternoon; which allowed the Saxon Raedwald, king of East Anglia, to retain in his church not only a Christian altar but an altar to his heathen gods; which encouraged the contemporary warrior-owner of the Derbyshire Benty Grange helmet to ensure his prospects of immortality by displaying both the emblem of a Christian cross as well as that of the boar sacred to the pagan goddess Frīg (or Frēo), may be recognised even today—some two thousand years later—in (for example) Central America, where pagan shrines surrounded by lighted candles are sometimes to be found within the very walls of Christian churches.

Then again the story of the Virgin Birth of Christ cannot be accepted as an incontrovertible fact, since it rests on a mis-translation of the early Hebrew Scriptures. Biblical scholars are aware that the Hebrew word in Isaiah regarding the prophecy of the birth of Christ means in point of fact a 'young woman' (there is another Hebrew word for a 'virgin'). But when the authors of the Septuagint translated the Hebrew word into Greek they incorrectly

---

[1] Frazer, *Golden Bough*, 361.

rendered it 'virgin'. Thus Matthew, when quoting from the Greek Septuagint, says: 'Now all this was done, that it might be fulfilled which was spoken of the Lord by the prophet, saying, Behold, a *virgin* shall be with child, and shall bring forth a son, and they shall call his name Emmanuel.' Now contemporaries would be well aware that a virgin birth was the expected prerogative of a deity and that the miracle of the Virgin Birth propounded by the early church was no different from that of the miraculous birth of the Phrygian god Attis who was regarded as having been born of his virgin mother Nana.[1]

The Christian account of the Blessed Virgin was therefore just another example of how the early church authorities sought to take over the traditions and rituals of its powerful rivals. Indeed, the rituals performed in honour of the goddess Isis 'with its shaven and tonsured priests, its matins and vespers, its tinkling music, its baptism and aspersions of holy water, its solemn processions, its jewelled images of the Mother of God, presented many points of similarity to the pomps and ceremonies of Catholicism.'[2]

[1] Ibid., 347.
[2] Ibid., 383.

FIVE

The triumph of Christianity

The earliest intimations of Christianity

What, then, was the special appeal of these 'mystery religions' of which Christianity was to become the most influential? The reason seems to have been the increasing sense of the sterility of the old polytheistic religions, and the need for a more personal faith emphasising both the moral responsibilities of individuals (with which the Stoic philosophy was the intellectual embodiment), and also the opportunity for attaining personal salvation. Christianity's monotheistic simplicity made for a closer personal relationship and sense of communion between individuals and their god. It avoided the exclusiveness of Mithraism, affirmed that everyone was equal in the sight of God, and opened its doors to the urban poor and slaves (Jesus's disciples were noticeably men from humble backgrounds). It appealed also to those amongst the aristocratic classes who supported the Stoic ideal of public service, and who with St Ambrose (c.340–97) saw it as the duty of all Romans to fight for the empire and the Christian faith against the pagan barbarians. Much of Virgil's writing had laid stress on the need to subordinate men's actions to the divine will, and this caused him to be regarded as the prophet of Christianity and was perhaps one of the factors which influenced Constantine in his decision to tolerate Christianity as consonant with the state worship of Sol Invictus.

Equally significant was what theologians might term the 'linear' rather than the 'cyclical' nature of Christianity. Christians believed in one figure, Jesus Christ, who was not like previous gods who were thought to have died and risen again in an endless cycle. They believed that the eternal God had uniquely revealed himself in the physical person of Jesus who had delivered a message of hope and salvation, had died on the cross to redeem the sins of the world, and would 'come again in glory to judge both the quick and the dead'. It was a theology, not merely of guidance for personal conduct but of hope and expectation. But the failure to provide the anticipated political Messiah led to a degree of disillusionment on the part of the early church as evinced in Bishop Eusebius's message to the Emperor Constantine (see above).

Nevertheless Christians steadfastly held to their faith, remaining mindful of James's words: 'Be patient therefore, brethren, unto the coming of the Lord' (James 5, 7). Two thousand years later we still await his coming.

From 313, the date of Constantine's victory over Maxentius at the Ponte Milvio outside Rome and the belief that this had been achieved as a result of divine intervention, the symbol of the *Chi-Rho* monogram (deriving from the Greek capitals *chi* (X) and *rho* (P) signifying the beginning of the word *Christos*, Latin *Christus*, 'the Anointed One'), which has been found on tombs dating from the first century AD, soon came to be regarded as the symbol of Christianity. It is found frequently in the Christian catacombs of Rome, and has come to light in a number of places in Roman Britain, and is to be seen on the Derbyshire Risley Park lanx (see below). The later Christian forms of the cross—the equal-armed 'Greek' cross or the 'Latin' cross with a long vertical—do not appear to have been used much before the sixth century AD.

The first appearance of Christianity in Derbyshire is a matter of considerable interest but about which there can be little more than speculation. Christianity had reached Britain by the second century AD, and St. Alban—a Roman citizen and reputedly the first British Christian martyr—is supposed to have died in 208/9. By 312 Christian bishoprics had been established at York, London and possibly Lincoln, and these sent representatives to the Council of Arles in 314. Thanks to Constantine I's tolerant attitude towards Christianity and Theodosius I's prohibition of sacrifices, the closure of pagan temples and the worship of household gods (391–2), the new religion was helped forward and enabled to meet the intense competition from other cults (such as Mithraism and Sol Invictus) in its early years.

Although Bede recalled that Augustine had repaired a number of former churches after his arrival in 597 very few clearly identifiable church buildings have been found in Britain which date from the Romano-British period. There are remains of small buildings with fourth-century Christian associations at Silchester and Richborough. There is also evidence of Christianity being practised at the Lullingstone and Hinton St Mary villas *c*.360, and occasional *Chi-Rho* symbols have been found scratched on masonry, plaster or on articles from the period (the Hinton St Mary mosaic containing the *Chi-Rho* monogram being a good example). An important collection of plate from a Christian shrine found at Water Newton has been dated to perhaps the first half of the fourth century.[1]

In Derbyshire a rare silver tray (15 × 20 in), known as the 'Risley Park lanx', inscribed with a Christogram has survived (Plates 13, 14). Found in 1729 in Risley Park this silver tray decorated with pastoral and hunting scenes may be dated stylistically to the fourth century AD. It bears the inscription

---

[1] P. Salway, *Roman Britain* (1981), 718–19.

EXUPERIUS EPISCOPUS ECLESIAE BOGIENSI DEDIT (*Chi-Rho*) purporting therefore to be the gift of a Bishop Exuperius to the 'Bogiensian church'. After being engraved by Stukeley in 1736 the lanx disappeared until 1991 when it re-appeared in London and was acquired by the British Museum. In fact, the lanx is considered to have been re-cast using the original Roman silver and is therefore a later reproduction of the original vessel. Neither the bishop nor the church can be identified with certainty, nor can its presence at Risley be explained.[1]

Romano-Celtic pagan cults lingered on for a considerable time (e.g. at Bath, where the temple of *Aquae Sulis* and the baths themselves lasted until the late fourth century, as did the two pagan temples at Silchester), and the Welsh monk Nennius speaks of Britain giving Christianity a 'tepid reception'. Christianity was evidently at that early period essentially an 'urban' religion (evidence of Christian activity comes from towns like Cirencester, Silchester and St Albans), which then became popular with a small section of the Romano-British aristocracy, namely the larger landowners, who observed it on their villa estates. Such men would have practised a faith which Dr Frend described as 'the Christianity of the Hinton St Mary and Frampton mosaics, which show Christ and the *Chi-Rho* symbol in the ascendant but traditional pagan mythology by no means excluded'.[2] The *pagani*, or country folk, on the other hand, were left to their own devices and continued in their old beliefs.

Place-name evidence suggests that Christianity had been introduced to north-west Derbyshire prior to the Anglo-Saxon migrations. The Celtic place-

---

[1] See G. Turbutt, *A History of Derbyshire* (1999), i. 241–2. For an account of the discovery of the original lanx at Risley Park in 1729 see C. Johns, 'The Risley Park silver lanx: a lost antiquity from Roman Britain', *Antiquaries Journal*, lxi (1981), 53–72. For the subsequent 're-discovery' of the lanx in 1991, and for an assessment of its history, see C. Johns and K. Painter, 'The Risley lanx "Rediscovered"', *Minerva*, ii (6) (Nov./Dec. 1991), 6–13. The current definitive discussion of the lanx is another article by Johns and Painter, 'The Risley Park lanx. Baugé, Bayeux, Buch or Britain?', in F. Barratte (ed.), *Orbis Romano Christianusque: travaux sur l'Antiquité tardive rassemblés autour des recherches de Noël Duval* (Paris, 1995), 175–89.

[2] W.H.C. Frend, 'The Christianisation of Roman Britain', in M.W. Barley and R.P.C. Hanson (ed.), *Christianity in Britain 300–700 AD* (1968), 2. The life of St Paulinus of Nola (354/5–431) is a revealing study of one such aristocratic Christian, a Gallic aristocrat, provincial governor and consul, wealthy landowner, and close friend both of Augustine and of the poet, teacher and Roman administrator Ausonius, who for some thirty years lived a life of pious asceticism (described by Augustine as 'Christianae vitae otium') adjoining the shrine of St. Felix at Nola in the Campania. We see here exemplified the traditional Roman aristocratic ideal of 'otium cum dignitate' in a Christian environment. And as he got older so his Christian faith deepened. After Rome was sacked in 410 legend has it that he spent the last of his fortune ransoming as many prisoners as he was able, and finally sold himself into slavery in Africa; but he was soon recognised by his captors and returned with honour to his home in Italy. As Helen Waddell recounts: ' ... on his deathbed this great lover of Christ and His church restored to communion all those whom for grievous error he had barred from the sacraments. Jews and infidels, says his biographer and disciple, followed him to his grave, weeping as for their father. It is the most fragrant chapter in the history of the saints' (*Songs of the Wandering Scholars* (Folio Soc. edn, 1982), 60).

13 Risley Park lanx, obverse (© *Copyright The British Museum*)

name element *ecclesia* ('church') occurs in three Derbyshire place-names. In two of these—the 'eccles' near Brough and the 'eccles' in the 'Ecclesbourne' near Wirksworth—the locations are places which are likely to have had a thriving Romano-British population on account of the nearby lead mines, where it may be surmised that many of the slaves or bondmen working therein would have been early converts to the faith. As Professor Thomas has pointed out,[1] the place-name 'eccles', deriving from the Latin *ecclesia*, does not necessarily imply a church building as such, but was also—and probably more often—used in the sense of a Christian congregation. The earliest church meetings were probably held in rooms in town houses and other such temporary accommodation. Later, small basilican-type buildings might be raised either within the walls of Roman towns (as at Silchester) or in cemeteries outside the walls over the tombs of early martyrs or holy men (e.g. as at St Albans), or again—in rural areas—in rooms in country villas set aside

---

[1] Thomas, *Christianity in Roman Britain*, 147–9, 262–71; K. Cameron, *Derbyshire Place-Names* (1959), pp. xxvii, xxi. We may note that for a 'church building' the Anglo-Saxons used the word *cirice* (ibid., 676).

14 Risley Park lanx, reverse (© *Copyright The British Museum*)

for Christian worship (as at Lullingstone). We would be well advised therefore to think of the three Derbyshire *'eccles'* place-names as representing the presence of Christian *congregations* rather than specific Christian places of worship. Their communal meetings might well have been at or near locations marked by ancient stone crosses.

Of the three Derbyshire *'eccles'* place-names Eccles Pike, a sharp hill feature to the west of Chapel-en-le-Frith, would have been an easily recognisable landmark for pilgrims approaching up the Black Brook, or alternatively from over Rushup Edge from the direction of the Hope valley. On its western slope was formerly situated a preaching cross of tenth (?) century date, perhaps marking the site of an original (and much earlier) cross (it has now been removed to the churchyard at Chapel-en-le-Frith). From here the early missionaries would naturally have been drawn along the Roman Batham Gate towards the settlement at Brough, where they may well have established another congregation and centre of worship in what was a thriving lead-mining area (the name 'Eccles House' half a mile south of Hope and alongside what was almost certainly a prehistoric trackway, suggests a possible site in the vicinity). From Brough the missionaries would naturally have taken the route of the Old Portway south to Wirksworth, close to the source of the river Ecclesbourne, to establish a third congregation in another area of lead-mining activity. A lane leading down into Wirksworth, carrying the Roman road from Little Chester via the Derwent ford near Milford, is still known as St Helen's Lane (the name of a favourite Roman saint who was the mother of the emperor Constantine). Another possible site for Christian worship was close to the hill feature known as Eagle Tor (within the parish of Stanton-in-Peak), which was earlier known as 'Egleston' (1529–32) and 'Eccles Tor' (1767, 1819). This site, on the edge of a prehistoric necropolis and close to the Old Portway, would have been on the route from Brough to Wirksworth.

Later history suggests that the Brough centre of worship may have been re-founded in Anglian times on the site of the present parish church of Hope. On the other hand the Wirksworth congregation could have been sufficiently well established to survive the two centuries of commotion after the end of the Romano-British period until a new Christian mission arrived in the area during the seventh century when Wirksworth again became a major Christian centre and the site of one of the earliest minster churches in the county.

Both cremation and inhumation were practised in Britain by the Romans: cremation was the traditional rite, and was generally observed in Britain during the first and second centuries; inhumation—partly no doubt because of Christian belief in the resurrection of the body—became more frequent thereafter.[1] There is some evidence of the practice of Christianity from Romano-British cemeteries. Inhumation (with occasional attempts to preserve the body, e.g. in lead coffins and sometimes encased in gypsum) without grave goods, and with the bodies facing east, is noticeable. There was no re-use of old graves, but—as in prehistoric times—there is a tendency for Christian burials to be grouped round an important grave (such as that of a martyr, bishop, or a family vault). On the Continent some early churches are known to have developed from the mausolea of prominent Christian families.[2] Regrettably, the number of Romano-British burials in Derbyshire is too few (and their date probably too early) to furnish any evidence of unequivocal Christian burial. Traditional Roman cremations have been found along the roadsides outside the *vici* at both Melandra and Little Chester, and many inhumations occur in the Little Chester cemetery area including a group

---

[1] Salway, *Roman Britain*, 693. As Professor Thomas (*Christianity in Roman Britain*, 228) has suggested, although 'faith requires Christians to view the dead body as a mere shell, of no import at all in itself, and reconstitutable instantly and wholly by Divine power from whatever gross decay time could have wrought, we can sympathise with the notion that a corpse neatly laid out and decently preserved in a stout container, so disposed as to minimus risks of impious displacement and possibly with external indices of name and status in society, would, in the nature of things, perhaps experience more speedy resurrection than a handful of scattered fragments housed within an insignificant urn and buried in a negligible pit'.

[2] Salway, *Roman Britian*, 731.

of military burials which can be dated to the early Antonine period. In some cases the remains of nails testify to the use of wooden coffins, but no deliberate eastern alignment has been observed up to the time that the cemetery went out of use in the mid-fourth century (indeed in many cases the bodies seem to have been aligned on the cemetery walls).

By the end of the Romano-British period the Christian Church had taken root in Britain and was even more firmly rooted in Ireland (where Celtic monasticism was beginning to flourish under the inspiration of missionary priests like Ninian and Patrick). But in Britain it was by no means securely established. Its chief supporters would probably have been members of the landed aristocracy, who were the intellectual elite at the time and many of whom were supporters of former pagan cults. Amongst the Christians a vigorous intellectual debate gave birth to Pelagianism in the first half of the fifth century (whose founder, Pelagius, had left Britain to study law in Rome *c*.380). Pelagianism was based on the principle of attaining perfection through the right use of free will (a notably Augustan and humanist concept), and this ideal—hotly attacked as a heresy by Christians (and by Saint Augustine, Saint Jerome and Bishop Germanus in particular)—probably did much to sustain the morale of educated leaders as Roman imperial powers faded from Britain. Nevertheless Pelagianism was condemned as heretical by the Pope in 418, but this by no means ended its attraction in Britain for we read that Germanus, bishop of Auxerre, came over eleven years later to preach against its continuing support.[1]

This mood of calm intellectual debate on the merits of Christianity as a new religion is very much in keeping with aristocratic scepticism of the last century of the western empire. Intelligent men were prepared to argue this out with the leaders of the church. A friend of St Augustine, Volusianus, 'lived in a circle which debated not only the old philosophical questions, but those doctrines of the Christian creed which presented the greatest obstacles to the reason. At one of these gatherings the difficulties of the miraculous conception of Christ, and of the Incarnation of the omnipresent Ruler of the Universe in a single human form, subject to all the changes, wants, and limitations of humanity, were raised. And Volusianus, in a letter full of deferential admiration for Augustine's character and learning, asks for some light on

---

[1] Thomas, *Christianity in Roman Britain*, 53–60. Heresy was a continual problem for the early Church. In the second century Gnosticism (based on the experience of a mystical and personal union with God) tended to undermine the authority of the Church hierarchy, and Irenaeus (*c*.130–*c*.200), bishop of Lyons, did his best to stamp out individual speculation and to demand unquestioning faith in Church dogma. For this purpose he wrote a large work, *Libros Quinque Adversus Haereses*, condemning all deviations from Church orthodoxy, and this together with the re-edited version of the New Testament commissioned by Constantine in 331 firmly established Christian dogma for future generations.

these puzzling questions'.[1]

Men like Q. Aurelius Symmachus or Vettius Agorius Praetextatus were far too inured to the old pagan religious tradition of their distinguished ancestors to pay heed to a new faith which seemed to them so far removed from practical realities. As Symmachus said in a speech to the emperor Theodosius:

> Each nation has its own gods and peculiar rites. The Great Mystery cannot be approached by one avenue alone ... Leave us the symbol on which our oaths of allegiance have been sworn for so many generations. Leave us the system which has so long given prosperity to the state. A religion should be judged by its utility to the men who hold it ... .[2]

Despite this plea, and fortified by the arguments of St Ambrose, the emperor stood firm. And in 392 a law was passed forbidding the worship of the household gods and all other forms of pagan worship. Notwithstanding the 392 law there is a record of many aristocrats deserting the Christian faith and lapsing into pagan practices. The situation was made more difficult for the church when Rome was sacked by Alaric in 410, when many people held that this was due to the state having abandoned the old gods in favour of Christianity. It was largely in answer to this that St Augustine wrote his great work *De Civitate Dei*.

The early church organisation was based on the bishopric, which coincided with the limits of a city or other administrative unit such as a large private estate. As civil government, law and order collapsed in the middle of the fifth century urban culture disintegrated and many of the provincial aristocracy, bishops and clergy fled from Britain across the Channel for safety (and were responsible for establishing the Breton community in Armorica). A few isolated Christian communities—including perhaps that at Wirksworth—may have survived, but throughout rural Britain the country folk would have continued to worship unmolested their local Celtic deities, some of which survived into medieval times as witch-cults. The continuing primitive rustic fear of the supernatural is illustrated by the survival of Derbyshire place-names embodying word-elements for elves (Eldon), giants (Thirst House), demons (Shuckstonefield), serpents (Wormwood), goblins (Puxhill), and—above all—the devil (*Deueleswode*, now Buntingfield, in Ashover). The 'Dark Ages' had set in.

---

[1] Dill, *Roman Society*, 14–15.

[2] Ibid., 30–1.

The mission of St Augustine

Some two hundred years were to elapse from the end of the Romano-British period until the establishment of the English church by St Augustine's mission from Rome in 597, but it was in fact an Irishman of the old Celtic church who was to be consecrated as the first bishop entrusted with the task of evangelising Derbyshire. The conversion of the Anglo-Saxon people of Britain to the Christian faith was by no means an easy task. As Einhard the biographer of Charlemagne wrote: 'The Saxons, like almost all the peoples living in Germany, are ferocious by nature. They are much given to devil worship and they are hostile to our religion … '.[1] The same would be true of the Anglo-Saxons who had settled in Britain. Place-name evidence of sites of pagan worship in Derbyshire may be recognised in Friden, meaning 'valley of the goddess Frēo'.[2] It was near here, at Benty Grange, that Bateman found the celebrated warrior burial with its boar-crested helmet dedicated to this pagan goddess, but also with a Latin cross supposedly in recognition of the new Christian religion. It is also a matter of some interest whether the garnet and gold filigree pendant cross found along with a circular silver-gilt brooch with cloisonné garnets set on gold foil (Plate 15), which were found in a seventh-century Anglo-Saxon grave at White Low on Winster Moor, represented the grave of a Christian convert. Some six miles distant is the hamlet of Wensley, whose name signifies a 'grove dedicated to Woden', who was traditionally regarded as the ancestor of the Mercian kings. Conversion to Christianity was therefore a formidable task. Nevertheless Christianity—through the combined efforts of bishops, kings and noblemen—gradually spread throughout the land. It countered the pagan belief in reverence for, and fear of, the dead, and the need for ritualistic propitiation in order to obtain their protection against evil, by preaching the sanctity of the dead, the spiritual intercession and protection afforded by Christian saints, and offered the ritual of Holy sacraments and festivals in place of pagan modes of worship. Instead of burial on the periphery of local settlements, Christianity brought the dead back into graveyards adjoining the new churches within parish communities, and instead of pagan grave-goods Christianity encouraged its believers to make donations to the church in the form of 'soul-scot' (a mortuary payment) and other dues, and to erect crosses as pious memorials. Pagan funeral rituals became assimilated into a Christian cult of the dead and relics of the saints, which led to the erection of shrines, the compilation of manuscripts on the lives of saints, and the start of pilgrimages. The shrine

---

[1] *The Life of Charlemagne by Einhard the Frank* (trans. Lewis Thorpe) (Folio Soc. edn, 1970), 36.

[2] Professor Cameron's suggestion (*Place-Names of Derbyshire*, 369) that Friden was associated with the goddess Frīg or Frēo has now been confirmed in a recently discovered charter of king Edgar.

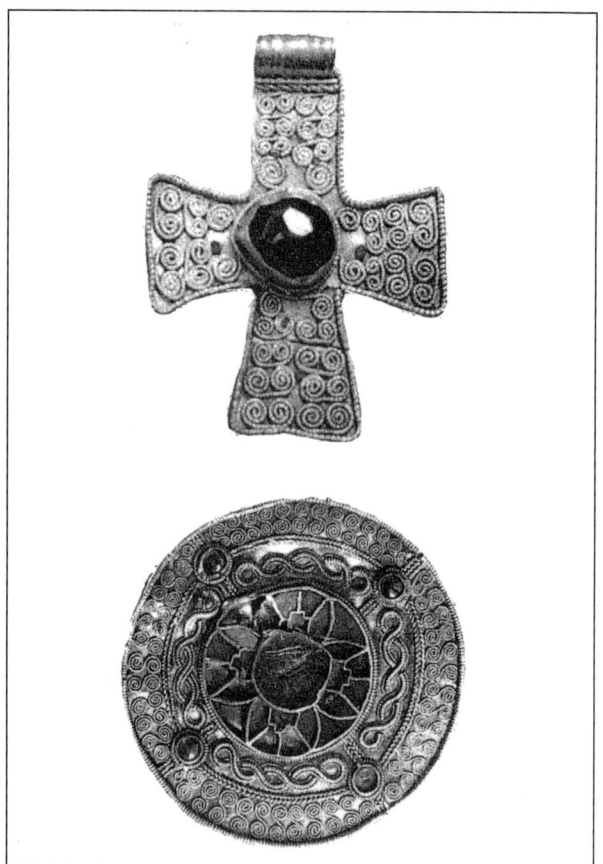

15 Anglian filigree cross and brooch from White Low *(Sheffield Galleries & Museums Trust).*

of St Wystan at Repton and of St Alkmund at Derby were both famous in their day and were visited by many pilgrims from all over the country.

The Anglo-Saxon church was born into a warrior society, had its own aristocratic heroes such as St Guthlac, and the message it preached of Christ the King and Judge, of the apocalypse and the day of judgement (all vividly featured on the Wirksworth grave cover—see below) was analogous to conditions of secular society with its temporal kings and its traditions of law and patronage. Essentially it offered a personal relationship and commitment between the worshipper and his god, and it provided a message of hope in contrast to the fatalism of early Germanic pagan tribes, and one which could readily be understood in terms of the structure of current society. But it was by no means universally accepted throughout all parts of England, and faced the same opposition from religious traditionalists as had been expressed at the time Christianity was introduced to the Roman empire. Indeed, the fact that pagan practices were still observed until well into medieval times, despite centuries of work by the early missionaries, is demonstrated by the need for the church to appoint penances for members of their congregations who sacrificed to devils, ate food offered in sacrifice, burnt grain for the prosperity of a dead man's household, or who indulged in similar heathen practices. Even today—unconsciously for most people—we still commemorate the pagan gods of our Anglo-Saxon forebears in the days of the week: Tuesday being called after Tiw (a god of battles); Wednesday after Woden (the war god); Thursday after Thunor (the thunder god); and Friday after Frīg or Frēo (the goddess of fertility). In this the Anglo-Saxons were only following the example of provincial Roman citizens (and continued to this day in French-speaking nations) whose names for Tuesday were *mardi* (after the Roman god Mars); Wednesday, *mercredi* (after Mercury); Thursday, *jeudi* (after Jove or Jupiter); and Friday, *vendredi* (after Venus). And of course the fertility goddess Eostre has achieved permanent commemoration because the early Christians chose to identify her feast day with that of Christ's resurrection from the dead (Easter). There are still many interesting relics of pre-Christian paganism in society today.

Christianity was first introduced into Mercia by Peada, son of the notorious pagan warrior Penda (who died in 655). Peada had been married in 653 to Alhflaed, daughter of the Christian King Oswy of Northumbria, and had been allowed by his father to invite four priests from Lindisfarne to undertake a mission to the Middle Angles of whom he was then ruler. After Penda's defeat and death in 655 at the hands of Peada's father-in-law King Oswy, Peada was made ruler of the South Mercians and established his capital at Repton. In 656 Diuma, the Irish leader of the four missionaries, was consecrated by St Finan, bishop of Lindisfarne, first bishop of the Middle Angles and Mercians, with the *cathedra* of his see at Repton, on a site which was situated on the edge of the low sandstone banks on the south side of the river Trent. Here he would have established a monastic community on the lines of the convent at Lindisfarne, and here, too, on the river bank he would no doubt have baptised his converts, as we are told Paulinus baptised his at Littleborough further downstream where the Roman road crosses the Trent.[1] It may be noted that the course of the river Trent at that period passed close to the north side of the church of St Wystan at Repton, but has since retreated half a mile to the north. Nevertheless the old course of the river can be clearly followed, and is bounded on its southern side by Monsom Lane which led to the old ferry at Twyford (the route to Derby formerly used by inhabitants of Repton until Willington Bridge was built in 1839). Repton, being the capital of South Mercia, as well as the site of a monastery with a growing reputation (and which was no doubt liberally endowed by Peada's successors), was soon to be adopted as the favoured burial ground of the Mercian kings (and so remained, even after Tamworth had become established as capital of Mercia at the end of the seventh century).

Of the religious community itself very little is known. In a Life of St. David the claim is made that David founded a monastery at Repton.[2] Since the saint died about 601 this would make it a late sixth-century foundation and a

---

[1] P. Hunter Blair, 'The letters of Pope Boniface V and the mission of Paulinus to Northumbria', in P. Clemoes and K. Hughes (ed.), *England before the Conquest: Studies in Primary Sources presented to Dorothy Whitelock* (1971), 5.

[2] H.M. Taylor, 'Repton reconsidered: a study in structural criticism', in Clemoes and Hughes, *Studies in Primary Sources*, 354 (quoting E.O. James, *Prehistoric Religion* (1957), 33).

natural focal point for Diuma's mission half a century later. On the other hand, Ann Dornier has made the interesting suggestion that a land grant (675 × 691) from a local prince by the name of Friduricus to Hedda, abbot of his recently founded monastery at Breedon-on-the-Hill, Leicestershire (and probably bishop of Lichfield in 691), might have been the original grant of land on which the monastery at Repton was founded, although the circumstances of Diuma's consecration as first bishop at the instigation of Peada would argue strongly in favour of an original royal grant of the site of his *cathedra*. Recent excavations by Dr Biddle have revealed traces of two seventh-century timber buildings at Repton which appear to antedate the earliest monastic buildings.[1] Whatever the facts of its origin there is no doubt that a double monastery (for men and women) was in existence there by the late seventh century when it was ruled by an abbess, Aelfthryth, during whose period of office the young Mercian nobleman, later known as St Guthlac (who died in 714), received the tonsure. In the seventh century the concept of the double monastery, for both men and women, had found acceptance in western Europe, with an abbess in charge of the whole establishment, most of whom were women of high rank and exceptional reputation (e.g. Hild of Whitby, Aethelthryth of Ely and Mildburg of Much Wenlock). These communities were an important feature of the early church and it is known that the sisters of Wulfhere, king of Mercia, namely Cyneburga and Cyneswith, founded a nunnery at Castor. Such religious establishments played an important part in society at this date, and provided openings for the talent of women of high social status. Monastic communities of the seventh and eighth centuries were free to follow their own rules, but under the influence of enlightened men like Wilfrid, Benedict Biscop and Aldhelm of Malmesbury the Rule of St. Benedict was widely adopted. Most of these early communities were however destroyed during the Danish invasions, and when English monasticism was revived in the tenth century the double monastery, as exemplified at Repton and elsewhere, did not accord with the higher standards of discipline, spirituality and celibacy then in favour.

Repton again features in the records under the year 714 when its abbess, Eadburga (or Ecburg), sent a lead coffin for the burial of St Guthlac of Croyland.[2] A later abbess, Cyneward, appears in a record of 835 as granting land at Wirksworth to Humbert, ealdorman of the *Tomsaetan*, on condition that he paid to Archbishop Ceolnoth an annual rent of lead to the value of 300

---

[1] A. Dornier, 'The Anglo-Saxon monastery at Breedon-on-the-Hill, Leicestershire', in idem (ed.), *Mercian Studies* (1977), 158. Excavations by Dr Biddle have revealed traces of two timber halls antedating this grant, which Biddle thinks may have been situated on the estate granted by Friduricus to the new religious community.

[2] There is however an element of doubt as to whether Ecburg was in fact abbess of Repton: see Biddle and Kjølbye-Biddle, 'The Repton Stone', *Anglo-Saxon Studies*, xiv (1985), 235 n. 15.

solidi for the repair of Christ Church, Canterbury.[1] The connection between the monastery of Repton and Wirksworth is of significance. Wirksworth (it will be recalled) was perhaps the only place in the county where Christianity may have survived from the Romano-British period, and its church was undoubtedly one of the earliest minster churches and was flourishing during the eighth century if not earlier. How the ownership of the lead mines came to be vested in the monastery of Repton is likely to remain a mystery. Cox stated that 'the manor of Wirksworth, with its valuable lead mines, was a royal gift to the anciently-established monastery of Repton, when it was first founded in the latter half of the seventh century',[2] a plausible enough suggestion but without any supporting evidence. As was the case with many other double monasteries the Repton mixed community does not appear to have survived the plundering of the Danish army in 873–4. However its church continued to be used throughout the late Saxon period, and a collegiate community was in existence there at the time of the Domesday Survey.

Diuma died within a short time of his appointment as bishop, and is traditionally said to have been buried at Repton. He was succeeded by another Irishman, Ceollach, who soon retired to Iona, then by Trumhere and afterwards by Jaruman. On the latter's death in 667 his place as diocesan was temporarily filled by the energetic Wilfrid of Ripon, who recommended that the *cathedra* of the see should be moved to Lichfield, which had recently been given to him by King Wulfhere.[3] In 669 Ceadda, or Chad (as he is more popularly known), was appointed bishop of Mercia and Lindsey by the newly arrived Archbishop Theodore and on his death in 672 was buried at Lichfield and later canonised. In 679 the enormous diocese of Mercia was divided up, leading to the creation of a separate diocese of Lindsey and later to that of Leicester. The see of Lichfield was left with the area of the present-day counties of Staffordshire, Derbyshire and Cheshire, as well as parts of Warwickshire and Shropshire. The line of demarcation between the sees of Lichfield and Lindsey (which constituted also the boundary between the provinces of Canterbury and York after the county of Nottingham was annexed to the latter province in 956) lay along what is now the Derbyshire–Nottinghamshire border, and the march with the see of Leicester approximated to the present irregular county boundary south of the river Trent. It was these early ecclesiastical boundaries which in the late ninth century

---

[1]. C.R. Hart, *The Early Charters of Northern England and the North Midlands* (1975), 102, although, as in the case of Ecburg (see previous note), the evidence that Cynewara was abbess of Repton is only inferential (Biddle and Kjølbye-Biddle, 'The Repton Stone', 235 n. 14).

[2] J.C. Cox, 'On an early Christian tomb at Wirksworth', in W. Andrews (ed.), *Bygone Derbyshire* (1892), 19.

[3] *VCH Staffs.*, iii. 140.

appear to have been utilised as the northern, eastern and southern boundaries of the territory of the Danish army which settled in Derbyshire, and thereafter to have become crystallised into the county boundary.

By the eighth century bishops had become substantial landowners through the generosity of kings and wealthy laymen, and some were bordering on the status of temporal princes. Their relations were being given positions of authority in the church as abbots and abbesses, and they were encouraged to endow monastic houses to which they could retire and where eventually they could be buried and prayers thereafter offered continuously for the welfare of their souls. A bishop of Lichfield had been given by royal grant two centuries or more prior to the Conquest the important estate of Sawley and Long Eaton in Derbyshire, and another had been given by the Mercian thegn Wulfric Spot (shortly after the year 1000) the estate of Bupton and Longford. The college of secular canons established at Lichfield by Bishop Aethelweald in 822 was succeeded in the 1130s by a cathedral chapter ordained by Bishop Roger de Clinton on the lines recently introduced at York and Lincoln. The canons were each supported by a prebend (a term derived from *praebenda*, meaning allowance for food, and consisting of a landed endowment), and the diocesan treasurer was customarily given the prebend of Sawley (which consisted of the ecclesiastical part of the original bishop's manor referred to above) for his maintenance, a practice which continued down to 1845. From the seventh century onwards, monasteries and minster churches were spreading Christianity in the countryside, encouraged by Christian Mercian kings such as Wulfhere (657–675) and Aethelbald (716–757). Apart from Repton, minster churches were founded on royal estates at Wirksworth, Ashbourne, Bakewell, Hope, Derby and Chesterfield. In the mid ninth century the minster churches at both Repton and Derby were the centres of pilgrimage to the shrines of St. Wystan and St Alkmund, respectively. Offa (757–796), as part of his political strategy, even succeeded in obtaining agreement from the Pope to the establishment of an independent ecclesiastical province of Lichfield (a move which was quietly invalidated within a few years).

After the initial destruction of many minsters, churches and preaching crosses by the Viking invaders at the end of the ninth century, during which the important minsters of St Wystan at Repton and St Alkmund at Derby were badly damaged (and circumstantial evidence suggests that the minsters at Wirksworth, Bakewell and Chesterfield also suffered substantial damage), Christian communities throughout the Danelaw were faced with the task of rebuilding their churches and converting the new pagan settlers. This process coincided with a wider movement of monastic revival and reform which occurred throughout Europe during the ninth and tenth centuries. As early as 734 Bede had complained of the deteriorating state of the Church in northern England: the bishops negligent, the dioceses too large for adequate supervision, the proliferation of pseudo-religious houses often ruled by laymen the conduct of whose inmates gave cause for scandal. The new reformers, amongst whom St Dunstan was the leading figure, sought to encourage the celibacy of monks, to order their lives in accordance with stricter disciplines, and to secure for these reformed houses adequate and inalienable endowments which would not be at the risk of reversion to lay patrons. The foundation of Burton Abbey by the wealthy Mercian thegn Wulfric Spot, and its endowment with extensive lands in Derbyshire, was spurred by this new movement for monastic reform. It should be noted that the earlier concept of double monasteries, embracing a community of nuns (as at Repton), had now fallen out of favour, their place being taken by colleges of male canons, and women of high status were encouraged to be benefactresses rather than participate in the new monastic reform movement. But the missionary work of the early monasteries and minsters brought forth fruit in that it paved the way for the founding by lay patrons of numerous parish churches on their estates from the tenth century onwards, which enabled Christianity to reach even the most isolated areas of the countryside. It had now become a truly national religion.

The minster churches

In the Romano-British period, during which Christianity had become the official imperial religion, it had been customary for each *civitas* capital to have its own bishop, priests and deacons. Christianity was then an urban religion, and people living the countryside were left to their traditional pagan and superstitious practices. After the re-establishment of Christianity in Britain, when most of the former urban centres lay in ruins, the church began to reach out into rural areas. Under Archbishop Theodore of Tarsus (668–690) a new policy for evangelising the countryside was devised. There was gradually established, under royal or episcopal patronage, a network of 'minster' (vernacular for *monasteria*) churches staffed by communities of clergy whose task it was to carry the Gospel to people in the surrounding *parochiae*. These 'minsters' were for the most part colleges of secular clergy who, as members of the canonical order, shared a communal life often under a quasi-monastic discipline such as the Rule of St Chrodegang (who, as bishop of Metz, had instituted a *decretulum* or rule for his cathedral clergy in about 755). They were to work hand in hand with monastic houses (usually subject to the Benedictine Rule) which also served as missionary centres. The minster churches and their communities thus became the spearhead of missionary effort throughout the country under the leadership of the local bishop, whose *cathedra* was at the 'head minster'. At this early period everything depended on the zeal of the bishop whose primary duty, according to Bede, was that of preaching. Few of the secular clergy in the minster communities were advanced to the priesthood, and as Stenton pointed out: '... the division of a diocese into parishes, each under the episcopal charge of its own priest, was still a remote idea in the early eighth century.'[1]

The impetus for the establishment of minsters depended in the first instance on the attitude of local rulers. Indeed, without their support it was improbable that missionaries could achieve very much. In Mercia (as we have seen) it was the result of Peada's conversion that presented the opportunity to evangelise the Mercians and Middle Anglians. The minster churches in Derbyshire were built on royal land and given endowments by the Mercian kings and sympathetic noblemen. While the Domesday Survey (1086) is well known for its haphazard listing of churches, most of the Derbyshire minsters may be recognised as churches of superior status by the fact that they have one or more priests and endowments of at least one carucate (Chesterfield is however omitted altogether, while Wirksworth is simply recorded as having a priest and a church). Domesday also shows them to have been built on the largest pre-Conquest royal estates, which after the Conquest are listed as royal manors to which were attached a number of outlying berewicks or areas of sokeland. Some of these territorial satellites later had their own chapels of ease which became daughter churches of the minster and were served by their priests, in much the same way as contemporary 'team ministries'.

Apart from the monastic community at Repton, which was the starting point for the Christianisation of Derbyshire, nothing is known of the religious communities at the other minsters. However, the creation at Lichfield in 822 by Aethelweald of a body of canons (11 priests and nine deacons) under a provost, suggests that he may have been introducing the *decretulum* of Bishop Chrodegang of Metz to his cathedral. If this was in fact so, then it may be presumed that his example would be followed by the minster churches within the diocese, and that the Rule of St Chrodegang would thereafter govern the lives of their secular clergy. Recent research has shown that the site of early minsters was not always coincident with that of the administrative centre of the royal estate which formed its *parochia*. Chesterfield is a case in point, where the minster church was built at the centre of the former Roman fort, while the administrative centre of the estate lay at Newbold (a mile and a half to the north-west) which is recorded at Domesday as the *caput* of the royal manor. Furthermore, minsters became not only the centres of ecclesiastical organisation and pastoral care, but not infrequently also of economic growth round which urban development took place in the late Anglo-Saxon period. Chesterfield again illustrates this process, where the urban development centred on the minster with the 'old' or 'weekday' market situated just to the north of the minster church, while the 'new' (and much larger) market grew

[1] F.M. Stenton, *Anglo-Saxon England* (1950 edn), 147.

up to the west along with medieval burgage plots. Newbold, the former manorial centre, soon lost its pre-eminence and never developed into a market town (becoming instead a separate manor).

The progress of evangelisation continued apace until the Viking invasions at the end of the ninth century when most of the original minsters appear to have been plundered and their fabrics badly damaged. The position was stabilised by 918 following the re-conquest of the Danelaw by Edward 'The Elder' (899–924) and his sister Aelthelflaed, and by the subsequent energetic action by Edward's son Athelstan (924–939) who defeated another Viking force under Olaf of Dublin (937). On Athelstan's death Olaf again invaded the midlands, but on his death two years later Athelstan's brother Edmund (939–946) succeeded in re-establishing his authority over the former Danish area (942). It was now that extensive re-building of the minster churches took place (no doubt with royal encouragement and support) and the collegiate church of All Saints, Derby (now the Cathedral), was founded on royal demesne land about this time by King Edmund (whose diminutive figure, bearing the title 'Eadmund Rex', kneeling with hands clasped in prayer, may be seen on an early medieval college seal).[1] There then followed a brief period of peace from Viking raids, and during the reign of Edgar 'the Peaceful' (959–975) there occurred a great revival of English monastic life and culture, which is usually associated with the names of St Dunstan and St Aethelwold. But the minsters once again suffered during the years of anarchy early in the eleventh century when they became subject to heavy imposts of Danegeld and also lost many of their landed endowments. All were relatively poor by the time of the Domesday Survey.

Minster churches assumed total spiritual responsibility for those living within their *parochiae*, and claimed the right to baptise and bury their parishioners and to collect various financial dues from the laity. Minsters were financed primarily by royal or episcopal endowment sufficient to maintain their religious communities, and seldom possessed less than one carucate of land (about 120 acres). They collected *Romescot* (or Peter's Pence) from the laity to forward to the papacy. They could claim the old parochial dues of *cyric-sceat*, or 'church-scot', from all freemen according to the size of their holdings, and since they had the right to bury anyone living within their *parochia* they could also claim *sawol-sceat*, or 'soul-scot', a payment by a dead person's heir for prayers to be said for the soul of the departed. From the latter was to evolve the medieval 'mortuary' present paid to the church (usually the second-best chattel). Plough-alms were also payable to the

---

[1] *DAJ*, xxvii (1905), 228. By the time of Edward 'the Confessor' All Saints had an endowment of two carucates of land in Little Chester and a staff of seven clergy. As a royal free chapel it was exempt from all episcopal control. It is possible that All Saints was a new minster church built to take the place of St Mary's, Derby, whose former endowments it appears to have inherited.

minster; for example, in the parish of Tideswell in the mid-thirteenth century the rate was ½d. for each plough-team, while in Bakewell a *ploughe penny* was due from everyone owning a plough within the parish.

Minsters later became entitled to tithes (which gradually replaced church-scot). The origin of tithe-giving in the church may be found in the Book of Genesis where Jacob, after his dream of a ladder ascending to heaven and hearing the voice of God above it assuring him of divine protection, makes a vow: '… of all that thou shalt give me I will surely give the tenth unto thee' (Genesis 28, v. 22). From this vow sprang a system of Hebrew taxation which was taken over by the Christian Church and lasted in England until a few years ago. At first a voluntary offering on the part of the devout of one-tenth of the produce of a man's land, payable in kind to a priest for his maintenance and for the relief of the poor and of pilgrims, it was soon turned into a compulsory obligation by the church authorities, and in the laws of King Edmund (944) tithe appears as an accepted tax on all land. When from the tenth century onwards, thegns began to found private churches on their estates, one third of the thegn's demesne tithes would be diverted from the minster to the support of the new church and its priest.[1] If daughter churches were founded within a *parochia* minsters were often reluctant to allow them to bury their dead in their own churchyards because of the loss of revenue that this would entail. They also retained the right to distribute the baptismal chrism to their daughter churches (the payment for which may be recognised in the later 'quadragesimals' paid to bishops by the parish clergy for the cost of chrism). Inevitably, therefore, the increasing number of church foundations and the granting of independence to daughter churches began to have an adverse effect on the minsters' finances.

It is to the minster churches that we must look for tangible evidence of early Christianity in Derbyshire. The art form which has best survived is that of sculpture, which was based on an amalgam of Celtic abstract design, classical imagery and primitive Christian models. Thanks to the durability of the material used—stone—a considerable number of fragments of sculptured crosses, grave covers and sarcophagi have managed to survive both the destruction of the Danes in the ninth century as well as the ravages of time, to leave us with a body of material dating from the period of the early missionaries up to the eleventh century. Derbyshire craftsmen were not of course wholly isolated in the field of sculpture, but were part of a wider Mercian regional artistic movement which was constantly subject to external, cosmopolitan artistic influences. In the early days these came pre-eminently from Northumbria (whose inspiration may in turn have come from Celtic Ireland), and it is not without significance that between the years 654 and 685

[1] J. Blair, 'Secular minster churches in Domesday Book', in P. Sawyer (ed.), *Domesday Book: a reassessment* (1985), 119.

Derbyshire north of the Trent formed part of the kingdom of Northumbria, which may well have facilitated the transmission of early Northumbrian artistic ideas. There was also a surprising degree of influence from Eastern and Byzantine sources on the Continent largely as a result of the close links between Offa's court and that of Charlemagne (whose gifts appear to have inspired the craftsmen who sculpted the friezes at Breedon-on-the-Hill, Leicestershire).

Derbyshire Anglo-Saxon ecclesiastical sculpture may be dated from after the second half of the seventh century when the conversion of the Mercian region to Christianity first began. The Wirksworth grave cover (Plate 16) may well be the earliest example of such sculpture and is both of exceptional interest and of national importance. Discovered in 1820–1 two feet below the surface of the pavement in front of the high altar covering—upside down—a stone-built vault which contained a large and perfect human skeleton, it had apparently been re-used as a convenient cover for this grave.[1] It was clearly designed for a tomb which was to be placed against a wall, so that spectators could look down on it. This is proved by the design of the sculpted cover itself. In form, it comprises a slightly coped coffin lid, divided lengthways into two compartments by a rib, each compartment being filled by a series of biblical scenes. We may reasonably assume that this was the cover of the tomb or shrine of an important ecclesiastic of the Anglo-Saxon church at Wirksworth, and which was probably placed against one of the walls of the chancel in the original Anglo-Saxon church. The grave cover or shrine is a peculiarly interesting piece of sculptural art and its iconography has been discussed in detail by scholars. In essence, the ten compartments into which it was originally divided would have represented the scenes illustrating important feasts in the then current liturgical calendar. The chief iconographical interest of the sculpture lies in the original central figure-scenes of both compartments, namely, those of the Crucifixion and of the Ascension. In the Crucifixion scene we see depicted, not the usual Cross with the figure of Christ upon it, but a plain Greek Cross on the centre of which is depicted the figure of a slain lamb. This at once helps us to date the work, since there were periods when controversy arose between the Eastern and Western churches as to how Christ should be represented in art forms, as a result of which church councils decreed that Christ should be represented in human form rather than as a lamb. Against this background the most likely period for the Wirksworth sculpture would lie between *c.*740–80, during a period of political stability in the reigns of Aethelbald (716–757) and Offa (757–796), which would accord

---

[1] The Wirksworth grave cover has been fully discussed in Turbutt, *History of Derbyshire*, i. 304–6. Since this account was written two further studies have been made of the grave cover: Jane Hawkes, 'The Wirksworth Slab: an iconography of humilitas', *Peritia*, ix (1995), 246–77, and Nessie Armstrong *et al.*, *Four Anglian Monuments in Derbyshire* (WEA Darlington Branch, 1996), 35–48.

16 Wirksworth grave cover *(Derbyshire Archaeological Society)*.

with the close stylistic parallel between the Wirksworth carving and fragments of sarcophagi found at the minster church of Bakewell. We may note also that by the early ninth century the figure of Christ was again being portrayed in Derbyshire Crucifixion scenes since both the Bakewell and Bradbourne crosses (attributed to this period) show images of Christ upon a traditional cross.[1]

The remarkable number of surviving crosses or cross fragments is testimony to the vigour of the Christian faith in Derbyshire, notwithstanding the Viking attacks. The carving is vigorous and natural, the earliest series—from the eighth until the period of the Danish raids in the late ninth century—includes the crosses at Bakewell, Bradbourne and Eyam (Plate 17), the remarkable 'Repton Stone' (a fragment of a high cross), and the stone sarcophagus (Plate 18) from St Alkmund's, Derby (now demolished). After the re-conquest of the Danelaw crosses again emerge: cruder in form, replete with Scandinavian motifs, and with an often incongruous mixture of Christian and pagan symbolism (as with the tenth-century crosses at Hope and Norbury). Grave covers of 'hogback' design, comprising a stone slab of pentagonal section in which the sides and slopes of the gable are carved with elaborate

[1] It is worth observing that in a very primitive tympanum in the Norman church at Ault Hucknall there is the representation of a lamb on the cross (above the figure of (?) St George fighting a ferocious dragon). This suggests that the tympanum is in fact of Anglo-Saxon date, as may be the very narrow chancel arch beneath the crossing tower. In the Domesday Survey (1086) Ault Hucknall is recorded as having a priest but no church. The latter may have fallen a victim of the Conqueror's policy of ravaging the northern counties after the rebellion of 1069, as apparently did Blackwell and South Wingfield churches.

17 Eyam Cross *(Derbyshire Archaeological Society)*.

interlace designs, and one end is adorned with the figure of a bear, date from the tenth century.

Of the surviving pre-Conquest ecclesiastical architecture in Derbyshire there is no better example than the crypt at the minster church at Repton, which became the mausoleum of the early kings of Mercia. This historic chamber (Plate 19), dating from the eighth century and probably built as the burial chamber of the Mercian king Aethelbald (who died in 757), was covered by a vault of nine domed bays, resting on transverse arches which spring from two pilasters on each wall and rest on four central columns which have spiral fillets and grooved capitals. Above this was later built (about the time of King Wiglaf's burial in 840) the sanctuary of a new church with central tower and western nave (Plate 20).

The parish churches

The author of an eighth-century *Life of St Willibald* refers to the fact that it was then customary in Britain 'to erect in the estates of nobles, not a church, but the standard of the holy cross raised on high'.[1] This would provide the setting for daily services of prayer. Preaching crosses such as these were part of the

[1] C.A.R. Radford, 'The church of St Alkmund, Derby', *DAJ*, xcvi (1976), 46.

18 Sarcophagus found in St Alkmund's church, Derby (*Derby Museums and Art Gallery*).

minster church system established by Archbishop Theodore whereby priests from the newly established minsters would go out into the countryside and preach to rural communities. The magnificent high cross at Eyam (Plate 17) may well have been set up as a result of an early mission from Bakewell minster. From the mid tenth century onwards, however, after the widespread destruction of minster churches and preaching crosses which followed the Danish incursions, and of the disruption of ecclesiastical organisation and monastic life that it engendered, a revival of Christianity took place which led both lay and ecclesiastical landowners to found private churches on their estates. Recent excavation shows that small private churches were still rare in 900, while a century later they had become common and from the 950s onwards lay wills increasingly mention bequests to local priests and churches.[1] This development, the second phase of the evangelisation of England (which was completed by about 1200), coincided with the gradual fragmentation of large royal and lay estates and the evolution of local communities under the leadership of numerous small landowning thegns. Hence the mid tenth-century laws of King Edgar clearly assumed that it was normal for a thegn to be possessed of a church on his property (even though it is clear that at that date some only had preaching crosses), and the laws of King Aethelred (1014) recognised the different types of church which then existed in England. Those listed were: the 'head minster' (or cathedral), the 'ordinary minster', the 'lesser church with graveyard', and the 'field church'. It was the last two categories which represented the proprietary churches now

[1] J. Blair, 'Minster churches in the landscape', in D. Hooke (ed.), *Anglo-Saxon Settlements* (1988), 57.

19 St Wystan, Repton: the Crypt *(Crown Copyright)*.

being founded by laymen on their estates. There were often disputes between the lay owners of proprietary churches and the minsters whose clergy claimed that the new churches were being established in their *parochia* and demanded that they become daughter churches and subject to their spiritual jurisdiction. This was the beginning of the process which was to lead to the fragmentation of the minster *parochiae*, and to the loss both of their former revenues and of their jurisdiction, neither of which were surrendered by many minsters (and especially by those appropriated by monasteries) without a determined struggle. In consequence of this new phase of church building the origin and boundaries of many parishes in Derbyshire may be found to lie in pre-Conquest landed estates on which the first churches had been founded, and the present parish of Stanton-in-Peak (which includes the village of Birchover) may be cited as an example of how an estate whose boundaries were defined as early as 968 became fossilised into an ecclesiastical parish.

The revenues of the earliest churches were derived from two sources: *oblationes*, or offerings, and rents from property bequeathed to them by pious benefactors. Pope Gregory had originally laid down the principles for the application of church revenues. These were to be divided into four parts: one for the bishop, one for the priest, one for the relief of the poor, and one for the upkeep of the church. No church could be consecrated therefore unless endowed with sufficient funds to ensure its upkeep and maintain its priest, but despite this injunction many village priests were exceedingly poor. Initially, the old minsters were endowed by royal or episcopal grant, and also received the parochial dues of 'church-scot' and 'soul-scot'. In the case of the later parish churches, where only one priest had to be maintained, the endowment, or 'glebe', was usually about two yardlands (some 60 acres) in extent. They also received 'tithe' (originally a voluntary payment which was gradually to replace the old parochial due of 'church-scot'). By the tenth century tithe had become a legal obligation. Where laymen had founded new churches with graveyards they were required to give one-third of their demesne tithes for its support and two-thirds to the old minster to which the new parish had formerly belonged. The foundation of a 'field church' (without a graveyard) had to be supported by means other than a share of the tithe, all of which had as usual to be paid to the minster church. By the time of the Conquest, as Stenton pointed out, most laymen regarded their manorial churches as being entitled to one-third of their demesne tithes, but they also claimed the right to devote the remaining two-thirds of their tithes, not to the old minster church but rather to any religious cause they chose—often, in fact, to the endowment of new monastic houses.[1] The founding of new parish churches was therefore to the financial detriment of the former minsters, but

---

[1] Stenton, *Anglo-Saxon England*, 156.

20 St Wystan, Repton: the Sanctuary.

was intended to take on and expand the work of evangelism which they had begun.

The old minster churches did not however suffer the loss of their revenues with equanimity. Those under strong patronage would, and did, defend their parochial rights against usurpation by builders of new churches. As late as the third decade of the twelfth century Chesterfield minster complained to the Bishop of Chester about the building of a new church (or perhaps the enhancement of an existing one) at Wingerworth within its *parochia* by Nicholas de Wingerworth, the lord of the manor, and obtained a ruling from the diocesan that the new church was to become a daughter church of Chesterfield, subject to its spiritual authority, and was to be served by one of its priests. Similarly the burial rights—and hence the mortuary fees—of the minsters were only reluctantly surrendered to daughter churches. A settlement between Chesterfield and its daughter church of Brampton in the thirteenth century allowed the burial of parishioners in the churchyard only on the strict condition that certain payments were made to the mother church.[1]

The parish priests were usually local men with only a limited education. The normal requirement for ordination would be some knowledge of Latin, music, arithmetic (with a working knowledge of the *computus* for calculating Christian festivals), theology and ecclesiastical law. He would be expected to be familiar with the service books (psalter, lectionary, gospel-book, missal, antiphonary and the like), and with the penitential, martyrologies and baptismal instructions. Many priests were married, and the tenth-century reformers tried to persuade them to take a vow of celibacy but without much success. Despite their worldly frailties the ministry of many devoted parish priests was to extend the Christian message still more widely throughout the countryside.

The situation in Derbyshire at the end of the first millennium was that minster churches had been established as focal points for missionary effort at Repton, Wirksworth, Ashbourne, Bakewell, Hope, Chesterfield and Derby. Indeed by the mid-ninth century the churches at Repton and Derby (St. Alkmund) had become the centres of pilgrimage to the shrines of the well-known Derbyshire Anglo-Saxon saints St Wystan and St Alkmund, respectively,[2] which had been constructed within them. As new converts were made

---

[1] Until the thirteenth century Brampton parishioners had to be buried at Chesterfield (where they maintained the churchyard wall adjoining their burial plot), but they eventually acquired the right to bury parishioners in their own churchyard in return for a regular payment to the mother church (J.C. Cox, *Notes on the Churches of Derbyshire* (1875–9), i. 115–16).

[2] It is unfortunate that despite the undoubted contemporary reputations of the two Derbyshire saints Wystan and Alkmund, so little has been recorded about them. According to the chronicler Florence of Worcester (d. 1118) Wystan (or Wigstan) was the grandson of Wiglaf (827–840), king of Mercia, who was buried in the Mercian royal family's mausoleum at Repton in 840. Wystan himself was murdered in 849 and likewise buried at Repton. The Evesham

landowning thegns started to build churches on their estates which became chapelries subservient to the local minster. Many of these were to become independent parish churches in later years. The second phase of evangelisation, with the relentless building of new parish churches, gathered momentum from the early years of the eleventh century and was not seriously disrupted even by the short-lived excesses of the period following the Norman conquest, the Domesday Survey (1086) recording (probably inaccurately) a total of 50 churches in the present-day county.[1]

The gradual acceptance of Christianity, and the rejection of pagan gods and superstitions, impressed upon society the concept of the sanctity of life, the virtues of maintaining law and order, and of personal charity as a means of attaining salvation in the next world. The latter in turn was a powerful factor contributing to the popularity of religious endowments amongst the laity. There is no doubt that by AD 1000 the Christian Church had become the 'established' religion in Britain, supported by royalty and aristocratic patrons alike, while superstitions and pagan practices—if by no means extermin- ated—gradually receded into the more remote country districts where they persisted for many more years.

In retrospect, the achievement of the early Christian fathers in establishing their 'new' religion was remarkable. To have convinced successive Roman emperors (with one or two lapses, e.g. Julian 'The Apostate') of the superiority of the Christian faith over other contemporary claimants by sheer force of argument (while quietly overlooking their belief that Jesus Christ was an earthly manifestation of Sol Invictus); to have recognised the public relations value of changing the dates of their liturgical festivals to coincide with those of age-old pagan festivities (celebrating, for example, the worship of Sol Invictus—the official state religion—but now with Jesus Christ assuming the place of Sol Invictus as the 'Sun of righteousness'); to have matched the symbolism of the Phrygian cult (adopted by Rome in 204 BC) whose devotees believed in the miraculous virgin birth of Attis (accompanied by the rising of a star), his death and resurrection on the third day (succeeded by the festival of Hilaria) and to have closely followed the cult's sacramental rites, and lastly to have fought so relentlessly against a multitude of heresies (e.g. Manichaean-

---

tradition is that he was assassinated by his relation Berfert; he was subsequently canonised (his festival being celebrated on 1 June), and his tomb thereafter became the object of great veneration for pilgrims until king Cnut (1016–1035) ordered his body to be translated to Evesham Abbey (Turbutt, *History of Derbyshire*, i. 291–2). Alkmund was a younger son of Alhred, king of Northumbria (765-74), and was killed *c.*800 at the instigation of Eardwulf of Northumbria, and he was initially buried at Lilleshall, Staffordshire. His remains were later translated to Derby where (according to the chronicler Ranulph Higden of Chester) 'he is famed for many miracles and is widely honoured by Northumbrians coming on pilgrimage'. His festival was celebrated on 19 March (ibid., i. 296).

[1] For a list of parish churches recorded in the Domesday Survey (1086) see Turbutt, *History of Derbyshire*, i, appendix 8.

ism, Arianism, Montanism), which threatened to weaken the force of the Christian message, was a quite extraordinary achievement. All this was accompanied by a sustained policy of evangelism which took Christianity from the Middle East to Alexandria and then along the entire length of the southern Mediterranean coastline (where, in former Roman cities such as Sabratha and Cyrene may still be seen the ruins of Christian basilicas), as well as penetrating to Asia Minor, Greece, Italy and throughout the whole of western Europe as far as Ireland. In due time Christianity was to provide the spiritual framework for the whole of western European civilisation (embracing its architecture, painting, sculpture, literature and music). Its manifestation in Derbyshire history is a reflection of this momentous spiritual movement.

Bibliography

Ashbee, P., *The Bronze Age Round Barrow in Britain* (1960).

Bateman, T., *Vestiges of the Antiquities of Derbyshire, and the Sepulchral Usages of its Inhabitants, from the most remote ages to the Reformation* (1848).

Ten Years' Diggings in Celtic and Saxon Grave Hills in the Counties of Derby, Stafford and York, from 1848 to 1858; with notices of some former discoveries, hitherto unpublished, and remarks on the crania and pottery from the mounds (1861).

Blair, J., 'Secular Minster Churches in Domesday Book', in Sawyer, P. (ed.), *Domesday Book: a reassessment* (1985).

'Minster Churches in the Landscape', in Hooke, D. (ed.), 1988, *Anglo-Saxon Settlements* (1988).

Blair, P. Hunter, 'The letters of Pope Boniface V and the mission of Paulinus to Northumbria', in Clemoes and Hughes, K. (ed.), 1971, *England before the Conquest: Studies in Primary Sources presented to Dorothy Whitelock* (1971).

Biddle, M. and Kjølbye-Biddle, B., 'The Repton Stone', *Anglo-Saxon England*, xiv (1985), 233–92.

Bramwell, D., 'Excavations at Fox Hole Cave, High Wheeldon, 1961-70', *DAJ*, xci (1971), 1–19.

Briggs, J.J., 'Notice of a discovery of ancient remains at King's Newton, Derbyshire', *The Reliquary*, ix (1868–9), 1–3.

Cox, J.C., *Notes on the Churches of Derbyshire* (1875–9).

'On an Early Christian Tomb at Wirksworth', in Andrews, W. (ed.), *Bygone Derbyshire* (1892), 19–32.

Dill, S., *Roman Society in the Last Century of the Western Empire* (2nd edn, 1919).

Dornier, A., 'The Anglo-Saxon monastery at Breedon-on-the-Hill, Leicestershire', in Dornier, A. (ed.), *Mercian Studies* (1977).

Frazer, J.G., *The Golden Bough* (Abridged edn, 1949).

Frend, W.H.C., 'The Christianisation of Roman Britain', in Barley, M.W. and Hanson, R.P.C. (ed.), *Christianity in Britain 300–700 AD* (1968).

Frere, S., *Britannia: a History of Roman Britain* (1978).

Grinsell, L.V., 'The Breaking of Objects as a Funerary Rite', *Folklore*, lxxii (1961), 475–91.

Hart, C.R., *The Early Charters of Northern England and the North Midlands* (1975).

Hodges, R., Thomas, J. and Wildgoose, M., 'The barrow cemetery at Roystone Grange', *DAJ*, cix (1989), 7–16.

Hutton, R., *The Stations of the Sun* (1996).

James, E.O., *Prehistoric Religion* (1957).

Johns, C., 'The Risley Park Silver Lanx: a Lost Antiquity from Roman Britain', *Antiquaries Journal*, lxi (1981), 53–72.

Johns, C., and Painter, K., 'The Risley Park Lanx "rediscovered"', *Minerva*, ii (6) (Nov.–Dec. 1991), 6–13.

Lethbridge, T.C., *The Painted Men* (1954).

Marsden, B.M., *The Burial Mounds of Derbyshire* (Author, 1977).
   'The excavation of the Roystone Grange round cairn (Ballidon 12), Ballidon, Derbyshire', *DAJ*, cii (1982), 23-32.

Naylor, P.J., *Ancient Wells and Springs of Derbyshire* (1983).

Porteous, C., *The Ancient Customs of Derbyshire* (1962).

Radford, C.A.R., 'The Church of St Alkmund, Derby', *DAJ*, xcvi (1976), 26-61.

Ross, A., *Pagan Celtic Britain* (1968).

Salway, P., *Roman Britain* (1981).

Stenton, F.M., *Anglo-Saxon England* (1950 edn).

Taylor, H.M., 'Repton reconsidered: a study in structural criticism', in Clemoes, P., and Hughes, K. (ed.), *England before the Conquest: Studies in Primary Sources presented to Dorothy Whitelock* (1971).

Thomas, C., *Christianity in Roman Britain to AD 500* (1981).

Todd, M., *The Coritani* (1973).

Turbutt, G., *A History of Derbyshire* (1999).

Wheeler, H., 'The Racecourse Cemetery', *DAJ*, cv (1985), 222–80.

Index